CUBAN SUGAR POLICY FROM 1963 TO 1970

HEINRICH BRUNNER

Cuban
Sugar Policy
from 1963 to 1970

Translated by
Marguerite Borchardt
and
H. F. Broch de Rothermann

University of Pittsburgh Press

Published by the University of Pittsburgh Press, Pittsburgh, Pa. 15260
Copyright © 1977, University of Pittsburgh Press
All rights reserved
Feffer and Simons, Inc., London
Manufactured in the United States of America

Library of Congress Cataloging in Publication Data

Brunner, Heinrich   birth date
  Cuban sugar policy from 1963 to 1970.

  (Pitt Latin American series)
  Bibliography: p. 159.
  Includes index.
  1. Sugar trade—Cuba. 2. Cuba—Economic policy.
  3. Cuba—Economic conditions—1959—   I. Title.
  HD9114.C89B77   382'.41'61097291   76-50883
  ISBN 0-8229-3342-X

Contents

Tables

vii

Preface

IN CUBA, sugar policy is tantamount to national development policy. This near equivalence is due to Cuban development strategy after 1963, which was designed to stimulate the development of the rest of the economy through the expansion of the sugar export trade. The expansion of the sugar economy was to be concluded provisionally by 1970, and thereafter its importance was to decrease in favor of manufacturing industries. Consequently, the present study has been limited to this period.

The development policy concept can be divided into three successive elements, which are the focus of the present analysis. The first is development strategy, the theoretical guideline describing the basic objectives and methods of the development policy within the constraints of domestic and international conditions. Within this frame of reference I investigate the significance of the sugar economy for total economic development.

This is followed by the concrete application of the model within the planning framework, its main object being the prospective sugar plan from 1965 to 1970. I try to reconstruct ex post facto the production and marketing plan.

To conclude, I study the third element of the development policy, the implementation of planning, specifically within the scope of the sugar economy. Here, forecast planning serves as the basis for a critical analysis, followed by a study of the repercussions of the plan on foreign trade and on the rest of the domestic economy.

CUBAN SUGAR POLICY FROM 1963 TO 1970

CHAPTER ONE

Development Strategy

CUBA'S DEVELOPMENT STRATEGY from 1963 to 1970 was rooted in the economic, political, and social situation of the country in 1963. On the domestic scene, the government, through its concerted redistribution policy, had improved the situation of the vast masses of the socially underprivileged. However, production bottlenecks had developed which threatened to deprive the social accomplishments of the revolution of their material basis.

This unsatisfactory situation was itself the result of a development policy which had its roots in Cuba's position on the eve of the revolution. The ideological guidelines of the new Cuban leadership supplied the link between underdevelopment and the rigorous measures adopted to overcome it. The causes of economic and social inequalities were interpreted in the light of the Marxist theory of imperialism, which led to correlated conclusions for their abolition.

To respect this link, the present study starts with an analysis of the factual situation of Cuba in 1958. It then describes the program of the revolutionary movement, which—by implication— envisions procedural political measures based on the regulatory policy of a socialist centralized economy to minimize the foreign dependency of economic development. However, until 1963 the application of this diversification policy only showed up the contradictions which arose from the island's productive capacity and the adopted strategy of balanced growth.

I will deal with these basic problems and expand on alternatives for their solution in a later section. The new growth concept, a special case of the model of unbalanced development, will be presented in the conclusion of this chapter in the context of Cuban reality.

3

Cuban Development Policy Between 1959 and 1963

Until 1963, Cuban development policy was characterized by a far-reaching transformation of the prevailing market economy into a centrally administered socialist economy. This entailed the reorientation of foreign trade from the United States to the Soviet Union. The situation of the island in 1959 was the reason given for the necessity of these changes. At that time, the country exhibited all the fundamental characteristics which constitute the definition of underdevelopment: a production structure geared to the needs of industrial nations, a high number of underemployed or un-employed, an extremely unequal distribution of wealth, and regional and technological dualism.[1]

The Cuban Economy on the Eve of the Revolution

With 44,218 square miles and 6.5 million inhabitants, Cuba is the largest and most populated Caribbean country.[2] It consists of an archipelago of 1,600 smaller islands and the long narrow central island, which stretches over a length of 745 miles. Among its principal geographic characteristics is its proximity to the United States, which has created a relationship between the two countries without which Cuba's development in the twentieth century cannot be explained.

The country is exceptionally poor in mineral wealth. It has hardly any source of energy other than hydraulic power, and intensive use of even this source is precluded by the island's topography. Among the rare mineral resources only the nickel deposits are worth mentioning; these are among the most extensive in the world. The paucity of raw materials makes it immediately clear that any economic development based on the extensive use of raw materials is possible only through foreign trade. Oil, metals, and their by-products, to mention only a few, can be obtained only on the world market. The obvious implication is that Cuba has to produce for export.

While the country lacks natural resources essential for raw-material-based industries, the climate and soil are exceptionally favorable for agriculture. The climate is subtropical and relatively even, and rainfall is adequate. The temperature range, coupled with the fertile soil, makes it possible to grow a number of crops even without special cultivation methods.

Because of these natural factors, the Cuban production structure has been geared since the beginning of the twentieth century to the export of agricultural products. Apart from relative cost advantages, the demand on the world market—or, more specifically, in the United States—led to a highly specialized production structure in agriculture. Sugar left its imprint on the total economy. It required approximately 80 percent of the cultivated land and employed one-quarter of the labor force. In 1953 sugar cane represented 13 percent of the gross national product, more than the aggregate of all other agricultural products. The sugar industry was the mainstay of the manufacturing industry, with a contribution of 5 percent. (See table 1.)

TABLE 1. Origin of National Income and Distribution of Labor Force, 1953

Sector	National Income		Labor Force	
	Million Cub$	%	1,000s	%
Agriculture			819	42
Sugar	274	13		
Other crops	259	12		
Industry			327	17
Sugar	130	5		
Other	387	17		
Construction	113	5	74	4
Mining	28	1	10	1
Transportation & communication	121	5	104	5
Other private services	896	34	532	27
Public services	140	6	96	5
Rentals	102	4	—	—
Total	2,350	100	1,962	100

Sources: National income: Harry T. Oshima, *The New Estimate of the National Income and Product of Cuba in 1953,* Food Research Institute Studies, Stanford University, vol. 2 (November 1961); sugar: "Memoria del Banco Central," quoted in *Cuba: The Economic and Social Revolution,* ed. Dudley Seers (Chapel Hill: University of North Carolina Press, 1964), p. 21.

However, the full impact of the role of the sugar trade is not illustrated adequately by these statistics. The health and growth of the economy were determined mostly by Cuban sugar sales on the world market. Almost every economic activity of the country was linked directly or indirectly to export production. When exports rose, investment activity increased and with it national income; when sugar sales on the world market decreased, the whole system contracted.[3] The business cycle of the entire economy followed closely the seasonal production fluctuations of the sugar trade.

Until the revolution, Cuba was the world's foremost producer of centrifugal sugar. As early as 1925 production reached 5 million tons, just below the yearly average between 1950 and 1960.[4] Statistical data support the contention that sugar production remained stagnant before the revolution.

Cuban sugar is derived exclusively from sugar cane, a tropical plant which requires a relatively hot and humid environment. It grows comparatively slowly at temperatures below 15°C. and develops best if the average temperature is above 20°C. Rainfall or artificial irrigation of about 1,200 mm is also of decisive importance. There is a close relationship between temperature and water: The higher the temperature (and consequently the evaporation), the more water is needed for the growth of the sugar cane. Insufficient water or excessive temperatures produce small, dry cane. Under opposite conditions the cane matures slowly. In addition, the soil must be able to retain adequate, but not excessive, moisture.

These conditions are so prevalent in Cuba that sugar cane can be grown without any special cultivation procedure, although when this is done, the yield per hectare is modest by international standards. Between 1950 and 1960 the yield fluctuated around forty tons, with deviations owing to climatic variations. For an improved yield, artificial irrigation would have been necessary to offset climatic variations. In Hawaii, irrigation spreads the harvest over the entire year. In Cuba, however, harvest time was limited to an average of five months because of the rainy season—light, to be sure—which starts in early summer. During that time the raw material needed for over 5 million tons of sugar—roughly 40 million tons of sugar cane covering about 1 million hectares—had to be cut.

Cane production in Cuba not only required extensive land use but also was labor intensive. In 1958 roughly 6 man hours were still required to harvest one ton; in Hawaii this figure was only 1.8.[5] On an average, more than 350,000 workers participated in the harvest; they cut the cane with a machete, a straight sickle, and loaded it on ox carts—few modern means of transportation were used—for industrial processing. Between harvests these workers were unemployed. Extensive land use and unemployment were closely correlated. Unemployment could have been eliminated by employing the farm laborers in nonseasonal agribusinesses. However, this would have required that land be set aside at the expense of the sugar industry, that cane production be intensified, and that manual labor be replaced by machines. In view of the low wages of workers who had to be paid only during the harvest, it was not profitable to make the necessary investments.[6]

In addition, domestic institutional organization was an obstacle to any increase in productivity. A production cartel dominated the structure of the Cuban sugar industry, protecting the small inefficient producer and discouraging the potentially productive one.[7] Each year the total marketable production was divided into quotas which were enforced with penalties. Since sales on the world market were subject to substantial fluctuations, the big producers set aside extensive land resources which they used only occasionally, while the small leaseholders frequently had to produce under very uneconomical conditions in order to retain their quota in the future.

After cutting, sugar cane is processed into raw sugar, which is then refined through an additional operation. Refined sugar suffers consistent discrimination on the world market; the importing countries prefer to handle the further processing domestically. Thus, to this day, refined sugar accounts for only a small percentage of Cuba's total production.

In 1958 cane in Cuba was processed in 161 mills with a daily capacity of 550,000 tons. That meant that for an average of 100 harvest days, or a daily cane crop of 400,000 tons, the mills were used at 70 percent of capacity. The most recent sugar mill had been built in 1925. The plants were old, although not technically obsolete, as there have been no basic technological changes since then. But the age of the installations precluded better use of production capacity owing to the need for frequent repairs. The plants were, in addition, equipped for a labor-intensive harvesting process in which only relatively clean cane could be processed. Mechanization of harvesting would have required substantial investments in the sugar industry.

Another constraint was the small collection range of the mills, which prevented them from operating throughout the entire harvest season. The collection range of a mill is limited by the means of transportation from the field to the processing plant, among other things. The traveling time of the cane must be kept to a minimum, since otherwise the sucrose content and hence the extraction rate decrease rapidly. The extraction rate is the ratio between raw sugar produced and the total of processed sugar cane, expressed in percentage of weight. Before the revolution, the average was 12.5 percent, quite high by international standards. This can be attributed to the fact that the cane was harvested only during its period of full maturity, that the harvesting was done overwhelmingly by hand, and that a well-coordinated organization insured smooth transport operations from field to mill. These three factors were to be significant ten years later, during the great effort to increase sugar production.

The Cuban sugar trade has been limited primarily by the world sugar market, where the regional deficit of industrialized countries is made up systematically by the surplus of the developing countries. Between 1950 and 1960 Cuban sugar represented on the average 30 percent of the total world export volume. But this figure does not give a clear picture of the importance of the world market for the Cuban sugar economy. Only a fraction of the total volume of sugar sold is traded between seller and buyer outside the vertical cartels. While terms of trade are stable in the closed system, the free market is distinguished fundamentally by wide price fluctuations. In marketing its sugar, Cuba used both systems. About 60 percent of her sugar exports went to the United States, the balance being offered on the free market, where her share already averaged 50 percent. This market interaction had the effect, on the one hand, of making Cuba economically dependent on the United States; on the other hand, the whole Cuban economy was affected by the lack of stability in the free sugar market. These relationships require further elucidation.[8]

World Sugar Production. The commodities traded on the world sugar market are raw cane sugar and refined beet sugar. Like sugar cane, sugar beets are grown in specific climatic zones, chiefly the northern temperate zone: in Europe, in the United States, and in the Far East. Unlike sugar cane, which is usually a one-crop culture, beets are cultivated together with other agricultural products, since they improve the soil for the latter or can be used as cattle feed. As a result, and irrespective of opportunity cost factors[9] (which, however, are controversial), sugar beets are being grown increasingly in industrial countries to satisfy their own sugar demand. Beet production is further stimulated by the desire to guard against the unstable conditions of the world market, although the possibility of increasing yields of sugar beets has been rather limited since the beginning of the twentieth century.[10] Sugar cane, on the contrary, is grown primarily for export, and the level of technology used in its culture varies greatly from region to region. Thus, substantial improvements in yield are entirely possible, particularly in the big producer countries of Latin America, because of the backwardness of present production technology.

From a global point of view, the function of cane-sugar production is to make up for the sugar deficit of countries that produce beet sugar. After World War II, it took five years for world sugar production to reach the prewar level of 25 million tons (see table 2). In 1960, the volume had already doubled and appeared likely to keep increasing at a similarly high rate. Beet-sugar production had increased faster during that period than cane-sugar production, first because it had been seriously affected by the war and made up

TABLE 2. World Production and Trade of Cane and Beet Sugar
(1,000 m.t., raw value)

Year	Production			Beet Sugar			Cane Sugar			Export		
	Total	Index	%	Total	Index	%	Total	Index	%	Total	Index	%
1935–39	24,850	100	100	10,055	100	41	14,525	100	59	11,920	100	49
1946–50	24,555	100	100	8,182	81	33	16,374	113	67	11,430	96	47
1951–55	36,172	147	100	14,535	145	40	21,637	149	60	15,314	128	42
1956	40,070	163	100	16,418	163	41	23,652	163	59	16,202	136	40
1957	41,186	168	100	15,821	157	38	25,365	175	62	17,246	145	42
1958	45,210	184	100	18,873	188	42	26,337	181	58	17,091	143	38
1959	49,544	202	100	21,238	211	43	28,286	195	57	16,651	140	34
1960	49,011	199	100	19,600	195	40	29,411	202	60	19,252	161	39
1961	55,352	225	100	24,585	245	44	30,767	212	56	22,254	186	40
1962	51,635	210	100	22,035	219	43	29,600	203	57	20,273	173	40
1963	51,155	208	100	21,833	217	43	29,322	217	57	—	—	—

Source: International Sugar Council, The World Sugar Economy, vol. 2 (London, 1963), pp. 230–39, 282–83.

for lost ground, and second because of the trends just described. With increased self-sufficiency of the industrialized nations, the proportion of total sugar production being traded in the world market decreased, at the same time decreasing the incentive to expand sugar cane production.

The two largest sugar producers, with a share of over 10 percent of the total volume, were Cuba and the Soviet Union. The sugar yield of both nations was below the world average (see table 3).[11] In the Soviet Union this was due mostly to climatic factors. While the agricultural yields had increased considerably by comparison with prewar results, this was offset by diminishing industrial yields. Cuba, on the other hand, while ranking next to last among the ten largest producers in yield per hectare (because of its backward production methods), could compensate for this disadvantage through above-average extraction rates.

While differing agricultural and industrial yield ratios to a certain extent reflect existing production methods or their improvement potentials in individual countries, they do not give any clue to production costs. In cane and beet production the input factors differ; and in both cases the valuation of the factor input can vary considerably because of different factor costs. Nevertheless, we can make the following observation: Cuban sugar production before the revolution was technically very backward for a large producer. That it could hold its own at all in the international marketplace can only be explained by low wages and cheap land—precisely the two factors which thwarted the modernization and humanizing of production.

World Sugar Consumption. Ever since its upswing at the beginning of the twentieth century, the Cuban sugar economy has been export-oriented. The market share of domestic consumption remained traditionally low. Consequently, the sales volume was dependent mostly on the development of world sugar demand.

Today sugar is a basic foodstuff in all industrial nations. While consumption in less-developed countries is still limited mainly to private households, in North America and Europe it has shifted increasingly to industry, that is, from the final consumer to the

TABLE 3. Average Yields of Sugar Cane and Sugar Beets, 1959–60

		Yield		
	Production (1,000 m.t.)	Agr. (t/ha)	Ind. (%)	Sugar (t/ha)
Cane sugar				
Cuba	5,506	40.3	12.6	5.1
Brazil	2,661	40.3	9.1	3.7
India	2,081	32.9	9.9	3.3
Australia	1,323	64.9	14.0	9.1
Philippines	1,261	64.2	10.3	6.6
Mexico	1,222	54.9	9.6	5.3
Puerto Rico	967	61.9	11.1	6.9
Hawaii	919	201.5	13.0	22.1
S. Africa	892	74.5	11.3	8.4
Taiwan	872	76.5	12.9	9.6
Dominican Republic	832	44.9	12.7	5.9
Indonesia	818	76.0	11.2	8.5
Argentina	808	33.7	8.1	2.7
World[a]	26,610	48.8	10.6	5.2
Beet sugar				
Soviet Union	5,090	18.1	13.7	2.3
United States	1,892	39.0	14.3	5.6
German Federal Republic	1,442	34.8	14.7	5.1
France	1,425	27.8	14.8	4.3
Poland	1,068	19.7	15.0	3.0
China	796	10.5	9.8	1.1
Czechoslovakia	789	26.0	13.5	3.4
Great Britain	747	31.3	14.4	4.5
German Democratic Republic	708	24.3	13.3	3.3
World[a]	18,394	22.3	14.1	3.2

Source: International Sugar Council, *The World Sugar Economy,* vol. 2 (London, 1963), pp. 235–37, 258–59.
a. World figures include data from countries not listed in this table.

intermediate processor. The upper limit of sugar consumption fluctuates around 50 kilograms per capita per year; this figure is considered the saturation point.[12] The level of consumption is mainly a function of income and sugar price, although regional differences in dietary habits also play a part. Deviations from these figures are found mostly in socialist countries, where sugar consumption is a function not of purchasing power but of administrative decisions.

The Food and Agriculture Organization (FAO) has sponsored a comprehensive study of the impact of income and price on sugar demand. This international comparison shows that in countries with low average per capita income or high sugar prices, the corresponding elasticity of demand exceeded unity. On the other hand, sugar demand was relatively inelastic in high-income countries or countries with low sugar prices.[13] However, the validity of this country-by-country comparison was affected by the necessity of converting the various currencies into a common denominator for both income and prices, a procedure bound to lead to distortions, particularly with inconvertible currencies. Furthermore, there is no doubt that income will affect elasticity of price and, vice versa, that price affects the income elasticity of demand.[14]

To circumvent these difficulties, the International Sugar Council studied the effect of a combined income and price factor on sugar consumption. Average per capita income was converted into sugar weight units at the local price of sugar (sugar income).[15] The common currency denominator was thus replaced by a weight denominator, and at the same time the differences in price were taken into account. The results confirmed the effectiveness of Engels' law. In the period after 1945, a sugar income of 4 tons per capita corresponded generally to a consumption of over 40 kilograms per capita, while for per capita incomes of less than 1.5 tons, consumption was below 20 kilograms. Deviations from these results were encountered mostly in countries with traditional cane-sugar economies producing for the world market. In these countries, consumption was higher than the sugar income would lead one to expect.

Table 4 clearly shows these correlations. The choice of countries listed was based on their volume of domestic sugar consumption, which is also determined by the size of the population. I did not take into account small countries with high per capita consumption (for example, Switzerland), or countries with large populations where consumption is low (for example, Nigeria). On the international scene in 1960, the United States was first among consumer countries, considerably ahead of the Soviet Union. The difference of almost 3 million tons was due exclusively to high per capita consumption. Other countries with high population figures were far behind because of their low per capita consumption. China, with a total of 1,170 million tons, was only in ninth place.

As to the future evolution of sugar consumption, it was reasonable in 1960 to expect that since per capita consumption was

TABLE 4. Average Sugar Consumption and Income, 1956–60

Country	Total Consumption (1,000 m.t.)	Per Capita Consumption (kg)	Per Capita Sugar Income (m.t.)
United States	8,240	47.2	8.91
Soviet Union	5,482	26.4	—
Great Britain	2,856	54.9	5.38
India	2,227	5.3	0.30
Brazil	2,177	33.0	1.19
German Federal Republic	1,680	30.9	3.58
France	1,447	32.4	4.41
Japan	1,263	13.8	0.99
China	1,170	1.8	—
Mexico	1,022	36.6	2.31
Italy	984	19.9	1.69
Poland	864	30.0	—
Canada	776	45.7	7.25
Argentina	707	34.9	1.94
Indonesia	685	7.8	—
South Africa	661	41.4	3.00
Netherlands	616	43.7	3.17
Australia	576	57.8	5.47
German Democratic Republic	564	32.4	—
Czechoslovakia	513	38.1	—

Source: International Sugar Council, The World Sugar Economy, vol. 2 (London, 1963), pp. 123, 269–71.

already above the world average in the European industrialized countries, further growth would be slow. Only in the Soviet Union and Italy was there a margin for increased demand. It seemed entirely possible that consumption in the United States had reached a plateau. In the other countries listed, with the exception of the net exporters of sugar, a substantial increase in sugar consumption was basically dependent on an increase in per capita income.

World Sugar Trade. Regional distribution of production and consumption determines the volume and territorial structures of the sugar trade. The distribution and organization of the market, as well as Cuba's place in this system, will be examined next.

The distribution of production and consumption by countries and groups of countries can be divided into three zones on the basis of common characteristics (see table 5). Zone 1 comprises North America, Western Europe, and Japan. Production is confined almost exclusively to beet sugar marketed domestically. Individual consumption is uniformly high, with consumption exceeding production by a substantial margin, so that about half of the requirements have to be satisfied through net imports. Zone 2 consists of the socialist countries. They, too, produce beet sugar for their own consumption, but by and large they are not dependent on net imports. With the exception of China, per capita consumption is only slightly lower than in Western Europe. Zone 3 comprises all cane-sugar-producing countries or regions, including Hawaii and, of course, Cuba. All these areas are either self-sufficient or are net exporters of sugar. In the first case, individual consumption is consistently below the world average; in the second case, it is above it.

In 1960 the total production of zone 1 was roughly 11 million tons of sugar and consumption about 22 million tons. More than half of the net imports went to the United States, but they remained remarkably stable throughout the period. The fluctuations of the negative balance of zone 1 obviously were caused by the demand of Western Europe, which varied greatly because of changes in beet-sugar production caused by climatic and other variables.

In zone 2, production and consumption of about 10 million tons each remained in equilibrium, and this relationship had not varied much in preceding years. This means that the socialist countries entered the picture merely as domestic trading markets for sugar; only the Soviet Union registered small net imports.

Zone 3 was the complement to zone 1. Production exceeded

TABLE 5. Production, Consumption, and Net Position of Zones 1, 2, and 3
(1,000 tons of sugar, raw value)

	1951–55		1956		1957	
	Units	Index	Units	Index	Units	Index
Zone 1						
Production	8,759	100	9,329	107	9,168	105
Consumption	17,863	100	20,344	114	20,151	113
Balance	− 9,104	100	−11,015	121	−10,983	121
U. S. balance	− 5,502	100	− 5,897	107	− 5,601	102
Zone 2						
Production	6,728	100	8,242	122	7,790	116
Consumption	6,657	100	8,040	121	8,581	129
Balance	71	100	202	284	− 791	1,114
USSR balance	− 591	100	− 369	62	− 675	114
Zone 3						
Production	21,008	100	22,771	108	24,594	117
Consumption	11,233	100	13,396	119	13,470	120
Balance	9,775	100	9,375	96	11,124	111
Cuban balance	4,981	100	5,394	108	5,307	107

Sources: International Sugar Council, *The World Sugar Economy*, vol. 2 (London, 1963), pp. 230–38, 260–65, 269–71; International Sugar Organization, *Sugar Yearbook 1960* (London, 1961), p. 111.

consumption by an average of 11 million tons a year, which reached the world market as net exports. Cuba's share of this volume consistently exceeded 50 percent.

It follows from this description that zone 1 had a monopoly of demand and zone 3 a monopoly of offer on the world market, and that trade flowed from Latin America and Oceania to North America and Western Europe. The net volume of sugar traded between these zones was equivalent to three-fifths of the world trade volume. This confirms that sugar traded on the world market was overwhelmingly cane sugar. Thus, the Cuban sugar economy was both offspring and cornerstone of the world trade, from which the socialist countries were virtually absent.

Since its origins in the sixteenth century, the world sugar market has consisted essentially of a conglomerate of separate markets for

TABLE 5 (Continued)

1958		1959		1960		1961	
Units	Index	Units	Index	Units	Index	Units	Index
9,333	113	11,238	128	10,688	122	13,503	154
20,975	117	21,218	119	21,746	121	22,502	126
−11,642	121	− 9,980	110	−11,058	121	− 8,999	99
− 5,770	105	− 6,032	110	− 5,979	109	− 5,797	105
9,937	148	11,366	169	10,260	152	12,376	184
9,390	141	10,086	152	11,424	172	13,830	207
547	770	1,280	1,803	− 1,164	1,639	− 1,454	2,048
− 227	38	− 359	61	− 1,102	186	− 1,900	321
25,409	121	27,464	131	28,248	134	29,642	141
14,628	130	15,099	134	15,594	139	16,469	147
10,781	110	12,365	126	12,654	129	13,173	135
5,632	113	4,952	99	5,635	113	6,414	129

the sale of colonial sugar to the mother countries. These closed systems were supplemented by a free residual market. This structure remained virtually unchanged until the twentieth century; a radical change occurred only with the territorial reorientation of the Cuban sugar economy in the wake of the revolution.[16] Today the "closed" markets are so-called preferential markets in consumer countries which grant the sugar-producing countries duty and/or price concessions. Since these are usually long-term agreements, the markets are stable. A classic example of the origin of a preferential sugar market in modern times is the expansion of the Cuban sugar economy for the U.S. market at the beginning of the twentieth century.[17]

As I mentioned previously, during 1956–60 the United States produced merely 2 million tons of sugar a year but consumed over 8 million tons. Of the required net imports, Cuba alone supplied an average of just below 3 million tons, and it was only because of the massive infusion of capital from the buyer country that Cuba was in a position to produce at all on such a large scale. In the end, the Cuban export quota was set permanently at 35 percent of U.S. domestic consumption.

Since U.S. consumption could hardly be expected to increase notably in the future, Cuban sugar sales to the United States had to remain stationary. The opening up of other similarly advantageous preferential systems (the United States paid 2¢ per pound above the world average) was out of the question. Great Britain, for instance, filled the considerable gap between production and consumption through the Commonwealth Sugar Agreement, whose purpose was to stabilize the sugar economy within the Commonwealth. A similar closed system existed between France and her former colonies within the Communauté, though in this case the mother country already had achieved a balanced sugar budget and, for the most part, merely handled the refining of raw sugar and reexportation.

The other major sugar consumers of Western Europe in 1960 were about to formulate a common policy within the framework of the European Economic Community (EEC) which was aimed at self-sufficiency of sugar production within the EEC. As in all other closed-market systems, importation of raw sugar was to be discouraged by means of subsidies and tariff regulations.

Another preferential market existed even before 1960 within the Council for Mutual Economic Aid (COMECON). The Soviet Union achieved a balanced sugar budget through imports from Czechoslovakia and Poland. From the point of view of world trade, these imports were insignificant because the sugar policy of the Soviet Union aimed at autonomy: The seven-year plan from

1959 to 1965 called for production to reach 10 million tons; the current twenty-year plan sets a target of 14 million tons by 1980.[18] With a population of 270 million for that year, this would amount to a consumption level of 50 kg per person.[19]

In view of the difficulty of breaking into these cartels, Cuba was faced with the choice of either selling more sugar on the free market or freezing production. The free sugar market ("free" because the price is the result of the unimpeded action of the law of supply and demand) is a typical residual market. In the years preceding the revolution, it was regulated by the International Sugar Agreements of 1953 and 1958. Contrary to the limits defined therein,[20] the free market handled the sale of sugar outside the cartels and the trade in refined sugar. As a consequence, the free market was a homogeneous market only for raw sugar, and then only for cane sugar, to the extent that it was not traded within the cartels.[21] In view of the specific quality of sugar in demand, only such a restricted market could be of any economic relevance to Cuba.

The demand came traditionally from countries without sugar colonies. The offer came from sugar economies whose (former) mother countries could no longer guarantee a sufficient outlet. In this way, Japan, the German Federal Republic, and Sweden bought sugar from Cuba, the Dominican Republic, or the Philippines. Like Cuba, other participants in closed-market systems tried to balance their sugar budgets in the free market; thus, on several occasions, the Soviet Union bought substantial quantities of Cuban sugar.[22] This residual market was exposed to wide fluctuations. Between 1954 and 1960 the turnover by weight fluctuated between just short of 2 million tons and 6 million tons, or 18 percent and 34 percent of the world trade. During this period the second Sugar Agreement barely succeeded in keeping the notorious price variations of the past within a range of 3.25 to 4.35¢ per pound by imposing sugar quotas on the exporting countries. These were then modified in accordance with necessary price corrections.

On the free market, Cuba enjoyed an oligopolistically limited seller's monopoly. From 1954 to 1959 the country sold annually between 2 and 3 million tons on the residual market, so that its market share remained in the neighborhood of 50 percent. This situation entailed mainly disadvantages for Cuba, however. When a World Sugar Agreement was in force, it was the Cuban quota that was hardest hit by the extremely wide margin of variation in the trade volume. During periods of unrestricted trade, the value of

TABLE 6. World Sugar Trade, 1956–61
(1,000 m.t.)

	1956		1957	
	Quantity	%	Quantity	%
Total world imports	16,202	100	17,246	100
From Cuba only	5,394	33	5,307	31
Closed markets only				
United States	5,897	37	5,601	33
Commonwealth	2,334	14	2,394	14
Communauté	742	5	865	5
COMECON (USSR)	84	1	19	0
All others plus				
refined sugar	2,444	15	2,568	15
Subtotal	11,501	71	11,447	67
From Cuba only	2,813	17	2,785	16
Free market	4,701	29	5,799	33
From Cuba only	2,581	16	2,522	15

Sources: For closed markets see International Sugar Council, *The World Sugar Economy,* vol. 2 (London, 1963), p. 164. Figures for "All others" are from Maryanna Boynton's estimates of the turnover volume of the free world market ("Effects of Embargo and Boycott: The Cuban Case" [Ph.D. dissertation, University of California at Riverside, 1972], p. 73). For 1960–61, Cuban exports to the socialist

sales fluctuated because of the extreme and short-lived price changes. This uncertainty was the reason given for the need of large reserves in landholdings which the major Cuban sugar companies set aside to guard against the ups and downs of the world sugar market. It also made investment decisions very difficult, since the anticipated return could hardly be estimated. It is significant that the world's most modern sugar economy developed entirely within a closed-market system with a favorable price structure (I am speaking of Hawaii and the United States); by analogy, there is an obvious correlation between the backward production methods of Cuban sugar and its partial marketing under the "free" trading system.

Table 6 contains an overall survey of the organization of the world sugar trade.

TABLE 6 (Continued)

1958		1959		1960		1961	
Quantity	%	Quantity	%	Quantity	%	Quantity	%
17,091	100	16,651	100	19,252	100	22,254	100
5,632	33	4,952	30	5,635	29	6,414	29
5,770	34	6,032	36	5,979	31	5,797	26
2,288	13	2,307	14	2,339	12	2,343	11
842	5	633	4	716	4	748	3
191	1	206	1	2,529	13	5,089	23
2,739	16	3,211	19	4,193	22	6,363	29
11,830	69	12,389	74	15,756	82	20,340	92
3,241	19	2,937	18	4,229	22	4,825	22
5,261	31	4,272	26	3,496	18	1,823	8
2,391	14	2,015	12	1,406	7	1,589	7

countries were included in the closed market. Free world market estimated by Boynton, ibid., after deducting cane-sugar exports to the closed market from total cane-sugar exports. Cuba's share calculated on the basis of *World Sugar Economy*, vol. 1, p. 126.

Domestic Repercussions. A first consequence of the priority given to the Cuban sugar trade over other sectors of the economy was that the better arable land belonged to a few large sugar companies and was therefore not available for other crops. The development of other agricultural production was thus strictly dependent on the sugar economy.[23] The first attempts at diversification were made during the period between the two world wars, when the sugar price had fallen to much lower levels than previously and had precipitated a serious crisis throughout the country. As long as exports declined, the offer of agricultural products for the domestic market developed and thus helped considerably to alleviate the import balance. When export demand rose during World War II, the emphasis shifted back to the sugar trade and, although renewed efforts were made during the years immediately preceding the revolution to broaden the basis of the agricultural structure, this evolution did not keep pace with the increased demand on the domestic market.

Professional and industrial development was hamstrung from a different direction. In connection with the quota system of sugar sales on the U.S. market, the two countries had signed a bilateral agreement in 1934 which remained in force, with minor modifications, up to the revolution, under which American imports enjoyed a compensatory privileged position—not only over other countries of origin, but also (by means of tax benefits) over local manufacturers.[24] As a direct consequence, Cuban industry was unable to develop fully in the face of powerful foreign competition on the domestic market. Even the industrial processing of raw sugar was discouraged in spite of the advantage of being on location, since the United States imposed a discriminatory tariff on refined Cuban sugar.[25] After a careful analysis, Max Nolff concludes that the Cuban industry was stagnating in comparison to other Latin American countries.[26] It was not in a position to utilize completely the potential of the domestic market, or to take full advantage of natural and human resources, and therefore operated so inefficiently that potential profits remained low and offered little incentive to invest.

Since the Cuban economy produced almost exclusively for the export market, it had to rely heavily on imports to supply the domestic market; before the revolution, these imports required about 30 percent of the disposable national income. A look at the statistics (see tables 7–11) will show that in this agricultural country the import of foodstuffs is the major item listed, followed closely by actual capital goods. About 70 percent of all imports came from the United States. Almost all plants and equipment of the modern production sector, as well as the principal primary materials, relied on American supplies, a fact that was to be of major significance after the revolution. The senior partner did not confine himself to trade vital for Cuba, but used cheap labor to establish some of his own efficient enterprises in agriculture, industry, and the service sector. These investments had a total value of $1 billion. American companies produced half of all the sugar, had a monopoly on the energy supply, and controlled communications from telephone to television.

TABLE 7. Agricultural Area, by Crops, 1959

Crop	Farmland (ha)	%
Sugar cane	1,108,200	83.6
Coffee	134,000	10.1
Tobacco	57,600	4.3
Cocoa	8,900	0.7
Others	16,210	1.3
Total	1,324,910	100.0

Source: Michel Gutelman, *L'Agriculture socialisée à Cuba* (Paris, 1967), p. 35.
Note: Pasture land for cattle-raising has not been included.

The single-commodity export economy burdened Cuba with all the principal features of an unbalanced economy, typical of underdeveloped countries. Production was dependent on an overpowering economic partner. Technological dualism was pronounced. Next to the few foreign or Cuban modern enterprises —which had the support of the infrastructure—were numerous small, labor-intensive operations. In the agricultural sector, large landholdings were dominant, leaving little room for development to the tenant farmers and peasant owners. Economic activity tended to concentrate around Havana, the port of transshipment for the United States, while the eastern provinces were neglected. Consequently, there also existed a regional dualism. Income distribution was extremely uneven, although there was a relatively extensive middle class, especially in the areas of industrial concentration.[27] In the rural areas, poverty, illiteracy, disease, and above all unemployment were rampant. The latter was mostly seasonal, like the production cycle of the sugar economy, but it extended beyond the agricultural sector, since the sugar economy was linked to a number of other activities. According to Castro's early statements, 600,000 workers—almost 25 percent of the available labor force—were unemployed over long periods of time.[28]

TABLE 8. Exports, 1958

Export	Million $	%
Sugar	594	81
Tobacco	50	7
Minerals	44	6
Others	46	6
Total	734	100

Source: Dudley Seers, *Cuba: The Economic and Social Revolution* (Chapel Hill: University of North Carolina Press, 1964), p. 19.

The Guiding Economic Principle of the Revolution

Analysts of the revolution largely agree on the symptoms of Cuba's underdevelopment,[29] in spite of a per capita income of $400.[30] There are, however, several schools of thought as to its causes and, consequently, the means of correcting it.[31]

For an understanding of government development policy, the mostly politically motivated analyses of the critics of the revolution are less important than the revolutionary movement's own interpretation of Cuba's underdevelopment.[32] The economic program of the "26th of July Movement" during the period of political rebellion (1953–58) confined itself mainly to criticism of the Batista regime and to demands for changes in the structure of the domestic economy. In foreign trade, a change of the commodity structure, but not of geographic distribution, was suggested.[33] Concrete objectives and measures were expressed in rather vague terms and were often downright contradictory.[34] A consistent theory of Cuban underdevelopment as the basis of future policy could hardly be attributed to the program.

Only later, after Cuba had aligned itself politically and economically with the socialist camp, was it said unequivocally that the revolution pursues "a development strategy aimed at transforming radically remaining prerevolutionary political and economic dependency to achieve independence and equality in international relations."[35] These objectives are based on a theory of under-

TABLE 9. Imports, 1955–57

Imports	Million $	%
Staple foods and		
nonessential food items	168	22
Textiles	59	8
Paper	32	4
Lumber	12	2
Chemicals	53	7
Fuel	55	7
Raw material	5	1
Semifinished goods	51	7
Other consumer goods	47	6
Machines	125	17
Cars	40	5
Others	107	14a
Total	754	100

Source: Dudley Seers, *Cuba: The Economic and Social Revolution* (Chapel Hill: University of North Carolina Press, 1964), p. 20.
a. Corrected by the author.

development which makes the history of the Cuban revolution appear consistent in its broad aspect, as far as the abolition of development-inhibiting institutional conditions is concerned. It also facilitates an understanding of the structural changes in the Cuban economy.

The tenets of this theory originate with Paul Baran and André Gunder Frank,[36] both representatives of the Marxist school. The analysis is based on the relationship between industrial nations and their client states, which makes economic development possible for the former but causes the underdevelopment of the latter. In a dynamic model of this relationship, the continued development of the industrial nations, made possible through the transfer of surplus capital, will aggravate underdevelopment, since the satellite works increasingly to satisfy the needs of the metropolis. This polarized metropolis-satellite structure not only leaves its imprint on international relations, but also exists on a national, local, and sectoral basis. It can be identified in the industrial nations them-

TABLE 10. Geographic Breakdown of
Cuban Foreign Trade, 1959

	Exports		Imports	
Country	Million $	%	Million $	%
United States	492	67	543	70
Latin America	10	1	80	10
Sterling Zone	48	7	37	5
Western Europe (other than Sterling Zone)	57	8	73	9
Other	127	17	44	6
Total	734	100	777	100

Source: Dudley Seers, *Cuba: The Economic and Social Revolution* (Chapel Hill: University of North Carolina Press, 1964), p. 20.

selves as well as in the underdeveloped countries. A class structure dominated by the middle class complements the system on the social level; and the interest of the entrepreneurs in the satellites, who are the beneficiaries of the domestic monopolistic structure of the economy, coincides with the interest of the colonial expropriators. In the present work I shall forgo a study in depth of the Marxist variations of the theory of underdevelopment; only the conclusions are of interest to us here.

According to this school, overcoming underdevelopment is more a problem of regulatory policy than of development policy.

The first requirement is to change the institutional support conditions which cement economic and social stagnation. Implied in this task, on the negative side, is the destruction of the capitalistic order and, on the positive side, the acquisition of political and economic power by the supporters of the revolution. The free-market economy, which rests on the principle of individualism, is replaced by a centrally administered economy which, during a transition period, leads inevitably to the acceptance of collectivism. The immediate objective of the revolution is to remove the built-in imbalance inherited from the old system, primarily to improve the condition of the disadvantaged segments of the population. Priority is given to redistributive measures and to a policy of full employment. Since both have to be accompanied by an expansion of economic activity if they are not to be carried out at the expense of productivity, a growth policy will predominate in the long run. Economic development, which under the extant production structure is restricted by close involvement with capitalistic countries, is possible only on the basis of economic independence or equality in foreign trade, if a recurrence of prerevolutionary conditions is to be avoided. This means that national production has to tend toward the substitution of imports in order to create domestically the material basis for economic growth.

With respect to physical determining factors, economic growth is basically a function of capital formation. Under this greatly simplified assumption, the rate of growth of the economy is dependent on the rate of accumulation which, complementing the rate of consumption, determines the national revenue from the point of view of utilization. The growth rate is thus indirectly a function of the level of supply of consumer goods to the population, and economic development may be expected to bring the greatest long-term advantages to the consumer if the latter voluntarily limits individual consumption during the intensive growth period. The assumption that a worker will surrender to the collective a substantial part of his production for the purpose of accumulation and will forgo immediate consumption presupposes that the work motivation be idealistic and not purely materialistic. At the same

time, in order to bring about a change in the material basis, a
prerequisite of economic development, it is essential that each
member of the new society undergo a change of consciousness to
attune the mentality formed by the prerevolutionary system to the
objectives of the new collectivist social order.

TABLE 11. Direct U.S. Investments in Cuba
(million $)

Sector	1929	1950	1958
Agriculture	575	263	265
Fuel and minerals	9	35	270
Industry	45	54	80
Services	290	305	386
Total	919	657	1,001

Source: Dudley Seers, *Cuba: The Economic and
Social Revolution* (Chapel Hill: University of North
Carolina Press, 1964), p. 16.

Economic Policy up to 1963

As I mentioned earlier, the Cuban revolutionary movement in
1959 did not have a clearly stated development program. This does
not mean that subsequent development policy was inconsistent.
The first four years of the revolution transformed Cuban society
and its political and economic international relations so radically
that if a formal program of change had existed as early as 1958, the
opposing forces might well have prevented the transformation.

The only firm commitment of the revolutionary movement was a
rigorous (by Latin American standards) redistribution policy; land
reform was initiated immediately after the take-over of political
power. The next step arose from the necessity of neutralizing the
opposing forces which turned against the reform efforts. This gave
an increasingly radical character to the revolution. It is against this
background that we must consider the progressive nationalization
of the means of production up to 1968.

The drastic transformation of domestic production conditions
went hand in hand with the shift in the geographic structure of

international relations. The policy of nationalization had hurt primarily U.S. economic interests. In retaliation, the United States and its Latin American satellites engaged in economic warfare. In view of these changed conditions, Cuba had no choice but to turn to the socialist countries for material and technical assistance.

Regulatory Policies. The first actions of the revolutionary government were aimed at eliminating those institutions which hindered the development of the country. Land reform was undoubtedly the most important step.[37] It was directed against both the large landholdings and the smallest enterprises in order to achieve a minimum size that would be economically viable. During enforcement, compulsory expropriations exceeded the boundaries of the decree and were directed against groups that opposed the new order. In 1960 the foreign sugar plants were nationalized, as were the domestic ones shortly thereafter.

The beneficiaries of the land reform were the small farmers and tenant farmers, but above all the state, which as early as 1961 controlled about 40 percent of agricultural production. The land that had been expropriated but not redistributed was reorganized after a lengthy experimental phase into "people's farms" modeled on the Soviet *sovkhoz*.[38] In the private sector, the farms were controlled by the Association of Small Farmers. These in turn were under the supervision of the National Institute for Agrarian Reform. In this manner, the government secured substantial direct and indirect power over agriculture.

In industry, nationalization of the means of production proceeded less rapidly but was more far-reaching. At the time of the take-over of the U.S. sugar companies, all other foreign industrial concerns, including service industries, were also nationalized. The Cuban enterprises followed soon, so that by 1963, 95 percent of all industrial production originated in government concerns.

Table 12 clearly shows the increasing power of the government over the economy.

By 1961 the transformation of the market economy into a centrally administered socialist economy was virtually accomplished, and the remaining task was to give it shape. First the need arose for central planning of most economic activities in order to overcome the intermediate phase of general improvisation. Foreign planning experts lent their organizational skills, but they were unfamiliar with Cuban reality so that their models were not adapted to Cuban requirements.[39]

Che Guevara became the real architect of the Cuban model of central planning. His main theoretical interest centered on the problem of consciousness-raising in a socialist system. He feared that the persistence of the old value system would impede the development of collectivist behavior during the social trans-

TABLE 12. Nationalization of Means of Production
(in % of production)

Sector	1961	1963	1968
Agriculture	37	70	70
Industry	85	95	100
Construction	80	98	100
Transportation	92	95	100
Retail trade	52	75	100
Wholesale and export trade	100	100	100
Banking	100	100	100
Education	100	100	100

Source: Carmelo Mesa-Lago, Revolutionary Change in Cuba (Pittsburgh: University of Pittsburgh Press, 1971), p. 283.

formation stage. Therefore, he wanted to abolish the old capitalistic categories, such as market, money, and commercial relationships between economic entities. He proposed to replace the former steering mechanisms with a model of highly centralized planning in which the principal basic entrepreneurial abilities were concentrated in one central authority. Instead of purely quantitative criteria, such as the profit concept, the leadership was to follow qualitative principles, such as "satisfying the basic needs of humanity." Elements of market regulations, such as cost and profitability, were to be retained only as index figures for comparison purposes, but not to regulate economic activities.[40]

Therefore, Guevara grouped the industrial units under his control into consolidated enterprises (Empresas Consolidadas) according to criteria of similar technology or similar markets for their output. The enterprises had neither financial autonomy nor individual accounting systems. Costs and proceeds were handled in separate accounts at the Central Bank. The managers only carried out instructions; they were responsible for the execution of the planning.

At first this "system of budget financing" was introduced by administrative decree according to a predetermined pattern, without prior analysis of the actual situation. Each enterprise received an identical organization chart; the central administration did not differentiate between them, regardless of their complexity or importance.[41] In the primary and tertiary public sectors, planning was to be decentralized and economic controls were to be given precedence over administrative controls. However, from the beginning, the self-financing system developed into a veiled system of budget financing and was abolished officially in 1965.[42] Up to 1963 these control models were still in an experimental stage, and the regulatory policies did not then disrupt continuity.

Structural and Procedural Policy. When it took control of the national means of production, the Castro government introduced a development policy which emphasized above all decreased dependence on foreign trade as a prerequisite to economic growth. The goal was ambitious: By 1970 per capita income was to be on a level with that of European industrialized nations.[43]

A prior condition to the achievement of this goal was a radical change in the production structure. If the single-commodity export economy and the resultant close involvement with the capitalist world market was responsible for the stagnation of the Cuban economy, the country could only free itself from this dependence by substituting its own production for the goods formerly bought on the world market. This strategy of import substitution made a number of demands on the individual sectors.

First, agriculture had to be diversified to satisfy domestic demand. This sector, which had been subject to extensive seasonal fluctuations, could thus be stabilized and would offer durable employment to the rural population. It was therefore decided to produce a number of items which had been imported previously and to intensify the cultivation of grain, rice, and tropical fruit. At the same time, however, the sugar economy could not be neglected because of its important role as a source of foreign exchange. In order to make land available for the new crops, sugar-cane cultivation had to become more intensive.

The center of gravity of economic activity was to be shifted to industry, which was given prime responsibility for economic development. The vigor with which industrialization was to proceed is illustrated by the objectives set for 1965.[44] Import substitution of consumer goods was also planned, as well as development of heavy industry. The necessary capital goods were to be supplied by the socialist countries.

During the industrialization stage, foreign trade had to retain its important position for the total economy. In view of the projected change of the production pattern, a shift in the type of goods was essential. Sugar had to remain the dominant export commodity, but imports of consumer goods were to be curtailed in favor of capital goods.

The geographic structure of trade had undergone a profound change as early as 1960. After the imposition of the economic boycott, the U.S. market was no longer available as an outlet for sugar exports or as a source of imports. The Cuban economy would have been extremely vulnerable in both respects if the Soviet Union had not stepped into the breach.[45]

We have already examined the problems connected with the marketing of sugar. There was no way for the Cubans to sell 3 million tons of sugar on the free residual market without provoking a severe price slump which would have reduced their import capacity substantially. Thus, the country was forced to find a new "closed" market. Among the large sugar-consuming countries, only the Soviet Union was in a position to import substantial quantities of sugar because of its considerable backlog of demand. At the same time, the vast economic potential of the Soviet Union offered the possibility of carrying out Cuba's ambitious indus-trialization project.[46] Cuba's economic calculations definitely fa-vored a closer tie with the socialist countries; this may well have exerted a strong influence on its ideological orientation.

The evolution of the Cuban economy up to 1960—before the radicalization of the revolution—was characterized by a general increase in economic activity.[47] This was due mainly to the government's redistribution policy, which stimulated an upswing in domestic consumption.

With the change in production conditions in the country and as a consequence of the American embargo policy, difficulties arose between 1960 and 1963 which called into question the initial suc-cess of the revolution. In agriculture it soon became apparent that the diversification policy was impractical. There was a lack not only of experts but also of organization. In particular, productivity was low in the new government-run farms.[48]

The FAO estimates that agricultural production rose to 109 index points by 1961 (1959=100), only to fall back to 77 points by 1963.[49] The sugar economy contributed decisively to this result. In 1961, 6.8 million tons of raw sugar were produced under favorable climatic conditions; then production fell to a low of only 3.9 million tons. What took its toll here was the setting aside of land for new agricultural crops at the expense of sugar cane production; this turned out to be an unprofitable decision in view of rising sugar prices.

Industrial production also caused difficulties. In the first place, it was impossible to install the plants from the COMECON coun-tries and to integrate them into the economy. As in agriculture, the technical and organizational background was lacking, since the supply of qualified experts had been greatly depleted by increasing emigration. Furthermore, it was soon discovered that the plants bought in the Soviet Union were technically obsolete, and the spare parts problem could not be solved through imports. How-ever, the crucial factor was the failure to achieve import substi-tution through the development of heavy industry, because the latter was itself highly dependent on imports.[50]

At the same time, not enough attention was given to existing capabilities. Investments and the efforts of the experts were directed mostly toward new projects. The problem of spare parts soon became so urgent that after 1961 some factories had to be cannibalized.[51] Thus, the old facilities could be used less and less while the new ones could not be set up for production.

As a result of the decreasing production of agricultural and industrial consumer goods, on the one hand, and the need for capital goods and raw materials, on the other, Cuban imports began to climb sharply. At the same time, Cuban export goods decreased because of the drastic reduction in sugar production. While commercial exchanges with the Western countries were still in balance, by 1962 there was already a deficit of more than $200 million with the socialist countries, whose share of the total trade volume was 85 percent.[52]

The technical side of the exchange of goods did not proceed smoothly either. With the government monopoly on foreign trade, one administrative body had to manage the task of coordination which had formerly been handled by a large number of contractors. In addition, the neighboring United States had been replaced by an economic partner with whom trade had to be carried out over a distance of thousands of miles. It is easy to visualize the difference: Formerly, a telephone call to Miami was sufficient, and the goods ordered soon arrived in Havana by ferry. Now a logistic mechanism had to be created to centralize the placing of orders. Long-range advance planning became necessary because of longer shipping distances and larger vessels. The port facilities proved inadequate and had to be enlarged. Warehouses—which previously were not needed—had to be erected. All in all, this reorientation required far-reaching new arrangements to replace a smoothly running, familiar system.

But even stepped-up imports could not satisfy the domestic demand. Government employment policy had brought about a wider distribution of purchasing power while at the same time, in 1962, the offer of mass consumer goods was limited. The government did not let the marketplace find its own level because it did not want to discriminate against the actual beneficiaries of the revolution from the lower-income groups. Therefore, consumer goods began to be rationed in March.[53]

At that point, the Cuban leadership (as well as the Soviet Union, which plugged the holes) had to recognize that the course followed hitherto had to be abandoned. In 1963, a reformulation of the development strategy of the Cuban economy began.

Development Strategy Until 1970

The revolutionary movement's analysis of the reasons for Cuba's underdevelopment and the concomitant determination of the various objectives of development policy had led to a concept that proved erroneous as early as 1963. Up to that time Cuba had adopted a development model which was meant to accelerate growth of the economy through rapid industrialization. The close ties with world trade based on the traditionally specialized production structure were to be reduced.[54]

The broadening of the production structure, justified on economic grounds, was hampered by a relatively small domestic market and by limited natural resources. Furthermore, the technical and organizational skills required for an aggressive policy of industrial import substitution were lacking.

Actually Cuba did not have to resort to the concept of self-sufficiency, for it had not been cut off from the world market. Quantitatively, the Soviet Union more than made up for the United States as an economic partner.

An attempt was made to formulate a development strategy, without changing the basic regulatory policy, which would be more compatible with the overall conditions of the domestic and new foreign economy. The theory behind this strategy can be illustrated by a model of "unbalanced growth" based on that of Albert Hirschman.[55] It starts from the basic principle of modifying the existing production structure through the one-sided development of a leading sector. The mechanism of backward linkage induces capital formation in allied branches of the economy or stimulates related import substitution. Such a policy tends to create a net-gain-generating cell around the leading sector and thereby contrasts with the more demanding diversification policy.

The effectiveness of this strategy rests on the fact that the (intermediary) market for the new production branches is already assured, thanks to the expansion of the leading sector. The expected returns from the leading sector itself must come primarily from the world market, in view of the limitations of the domestic market. This reliance is also due to the fact that, as an immediate consequence of the growth of the leading sector, imports of needed inputs increase, as do imports of capital goods that serve in their substitution, at a later stage. These imports have to be financed, so the pressure to increase exports is strong.

Cuba decided in favor of an economic development model based on these considerations.[56] The specialized production pattern imposed by the nature of the island and by global economic conditions resulted in the one-sided furtherance of the sugar economy. The choice of the leading sector was influenced mainly by the following considerations: Traditionally, Cuba was familiar with sugar production. There was enough manpower to grow sugar cane and to produce raw sugar industrially. Soil conditions and climate lent themselves to sugar cane growing. The existing capacity had proved adequate in 1952 for the industrial production of over 7 million tons of raw sugar. In spite of backward production techniques, sugar technology was relatively well developed.

Cuba's economic integration into the foreign trade system of the socialist countries was to provide stable markets for increased production, with favorable terms of trade. This economic interrelation proceeded from the assumption that cost advantages existed in Cuba for sugar production and in the socialist countries for the production of capital and consumer goods.[57] Unlike Cuba's foreign trade relations before the revolution, which had a similar structure of goods, the commercial exchanges with the socialist countries, thanks to a high price for sugar, were to be characterized by terms of trade allowing the exchange of "equivalent value for equivalent value."[58]

A further argument in support of the expansion of sugar production was that the excess capacity seemed to make such an expansion possible with relatively small investment expenditures. The marginal capital input efficiency was less favorable in the case of other potential export goods, namely nickel, because of the long-range nature of required investments.

Expansion of the sugar economy also opened up favorable prospects as a starting point for industrialization. To be sure, the increased demand of capital goods for sugar production would stimulate additional imports, but ultimately it would promote the development of domestic ancillary industries. Because of the large production and consequent high demand, it seemed likely that the criteria of minimum profitable size could be met in at least some supply sectors. In addition, the production of raw sugar, according to the theory of forward linkage, should stimulate other industrial activities for the further processing of the main product and of its by-products. In particular, there was the possibility of refining the raw sugar in a satellite industry.

Since the results of the diversification of agriculture had been unfavorable from the point of view of comparative cost advantages, the balance of agricultural activity was to concentrate on cattle-raising and on crops that could become competitive on the world market. Cattle-breeding was intended primarily to supply the domestic market, while the growing of tropical fruit was to supplement exports.

The role of industry was limited in the short run to making the widest possible use of existing capacities. In the long run, its development was to result from the expansion of agriculture. The interaction of the two sectors was to be intensified until the whole agroindustrial net-gain-generating cell could be consolidated fully. Sugar production, which belongs to both agriculture and industry, already provided the necessary framework for this structure.

While exporting the additional output of the final product was emphasized, the disposable final product—after completion of all foreign trade transactions—was to be used above all for capital formation. It followed that the consumer quota would have to be lowered concurrently, thereby postponing to an even more distant future the basic objective of the Cuban economic policy, improvement of the standard of living.

Unlike the import substitution policy of previous years, this development strategy took into account the nature of the island, its actual production capabilities, and above all the new potential of foreign trade. It promised a more secure, though slower, growth because the chosen road of development was leading toward a consistent production pattern which presented itself as the most economic alternative solution within the large economic sphere of the socialist countries.

The key to a successful realization of this economic model was to be sought in Havana as well as in Moscow. The Cubans had to do their part to increase sugar production drastically, while the Soviet Union had to guarantee the market and to supply Cuba with the essential capital and consumer goods.

Already in the spring of 1963, after close consultation with the Soviet Union, Castro announced the production goal of 10 million tons of raw sugar for 1970.[59] To him, the achievement of this ambitious goal was closely bound up with the fate of the revolution, and he therefore endowed the development strategy with a political content that far exceeded its purely economic significance.

CHAPTER TWO

Economic Planning

The Planning Problem

THE STRATEGY of unbalanced growth adopted in Cuba after 1963 called for one-sided, preferential development of agriculture as the leading sector of the total economy in order to stimulate industrialization. This presented a number of problems in application as part of an overall plan. The intention was to finance the import of capital goods by expanding export-oriented sugar production, using the capital goods for import substitution of intermediate and final consumption goods. It was essential to find a local market for this domestic production, a market which first had to be established through the creation of an agroindustrial net-gain-generating cell—thereby closing the circle.

The point of departure for this growth spiral was the agricultural production of sugar cane. As will be explained in connection with the sugar forecast plan, it was difficult to formulate directives for production planning even during this early phase because the comparatively backward production technique left the output of sugar cane dependent on exogenous variables which were difficult to predict. Climatic conditions ought to be mentioned first. Their consequences not only were felt in the cane-processing industry, but also influenced the activity of all branches of the economy related to sugar.

The difficulty of planning for the economy as a whole because of the instability of cane production became even more acute during the next step, that of export sales. In Cuba's export-oriented production structure, the maintenance of production and consumption remained highly dependent on import capacity, which was only partly determined by the volume of exports. More important were the terms of trade. These affected not only prices, but also—and this was particularly relevant for Cuba—the possibility of access to Western import markets.

Because of the dominant position of the export economy, the number and importance of its exogenous factors of instability inevitably affected other economic activities. Consequently it was extremely difficult to impose an overall plan. Medium- or long-range planning of overall economic development in particular could be no more than forecasts. Therefore, the attempt was made in Cuba to draw up medium-range specific plans for individual sectors of the economy. The most important of these was the prospective sugar plan of 1965–70. Its fulfillment determined overall yearly planning, because sugar production, together with the foreign trade agreements between Cuba and the socialist countries, served as index variables for the yearly import capacity. The availability of primary, intermediary, and final import goods was in turn the most important general factor in determining the production, consumption, and investments of the economy as a whole.[1] In the following pages, the analysis of the prospective sugar plan will be highlighted, since it is the key to understanding Cuban economic development until 1970.

The Prospective Sugar Plan from 1965 to 1970

The prospective sugar plan has never been published in detail or in a consistent form. Only partial information is available, so it is questionable whether a comprehensive version ever existed.[2] There is, then, no solution but to reconstruct the framework of the plan ex post facto from its individual parts and then to resolve any inconsistencies through the use of controlled deductive assumptions.

Because it is not easy to create a whole from the numerous fragments at hand, my description of the sugar plan is limited to selected variables. This will cause some oversimplifications but will make it possible to create an overall picture. I shall discuss first the subordinate partial goals that were set to reach the production and sale of 10 million tons by 1970, continuing with a study of investment measures and their financing.

Planning Variables and Goals Until 1970

As a first step, it seems logical to divide the sugar plan, for analytical purposes, into a quantity plan and a monetary value (financial) plan. Both plans are further subdivided into production and marketing components.

The purposes in discussing quantity planning are to introduce the individual production variables and the marketing variables based thereon, to retain their initial values as a planning base, to quantify the planning goals for 1970, and to extrapolate individual target figures for each year of the plan.

Quantity Planning in the Production Field. The main features of Cuban sugar production have already been touched upon. Proceeding from them, the following variables will be used in the production plan:

S = raw sugar production, in tons
C = sugar cane production, in tons
A = harvest area, in hectares
P = industrial processing capacity of C per day, in tons per day
p = average utilization of P during harvest, in percentage
l = productivity of labor, or C per day per harvest worker, in tons per day per worker

Five additional variables can be determined endogenously from these basic indicators:

$i = S/C$ = industrial yield, in percentage
$a = C/A$ = agricultural yield, in tons per hectare
$c = \dfrac{P \cdot p}{100}$ = cane harvest and cane processing per day, in tons per day
$H = C/c$ = average length of harvest, in days
$N = c/l$ = average number of harvest workers, in workers

If we know the basic values and rates of increase until 1970 for these indicators, the production quantity plan can be calculated.

The main point now is to become fully conversant with these variables and to justify their selection. To this end a brief recapitulation follows: Raw sugar is extracted industrially from sugar cane. In Cuba before the revolution, the industrial yield amounted to about 12.5 percent of weight for an average production of raw sugar of 5 million tons. This means that more than 40 million tons of sugar cane had to be harvested and processed. On the basis of an agricultural yield of 40 tons per hectare, this production required a land area of at least 1 million hectares.

The three physical variables, final product (S), raw material (C), and land area (A), as well as the parameters which establish the relationships among them, (a and i), form the framework of the production plan. We may assume that the Cuban planners expected to harvest in 1964—the base year—a total of 45 million tons of sugar cane from a cultivated area of 1 million hectares and to extract from it 5.6 million tons of raw sugar. The corresponding base values of agricultural and industrial yields were thus 45 tons per hectare and 12.5 percent.[3] The input of the other primary indicators is also of interest. Sugar production is labor intensive in its agricultural stage, but capital intensive at the industrial processing stage. Consequently, the other variables to be considered are the number of seasonal harvest workers (N), as well as the required industrial capacity (P), while the capital input for the cultivation of sugar cane and the labor input in the sugar industry will not be considered for the time being.

The requirements of manpower and of plant capacity are determined endogenously by the supply of sugar cane. The harvest season (H) is an additional index variable.[4] The input of the two primary factors is thus controlled by the average daily harvest performance (c); the corresponding parameters are the average daily performance per worker (l) and the average daily utilization of industrial processing capacity (p).

Not only is the length of the harvest season important in determining manpower and capacity, it is also an index variable of industrial and agricultural yields. Usually, the Cuban sugar harvest starts in November with the "little *zafra*" in but a fraction of the fields, while the real harvest begins only in January and lasts at most until July. Sugar cane should be cut when it reaches its highest degree of maturity. This can be maintained throughout the normal harvest season by the use of staggered planting and different varieties of cane.[5] If the harvest season is lengthened, inevitably some cane is cut before it has reached the optimum degree of maturity or after it has reached its prime. In the first case both the agricultural and industrial yields are reduced, whereas in the second case only the industrial extraction rate decreases, since although there is no weight loss the sucrose content of the cane diminishes.

In order to understand the base data for the other variables, it must be assumed that the daily industrial plant capacity in 1964 was sufficient for the processing of 550,000 tons of sugar cane.[6] However, this is a theoretical figure of which, because of the age of the plants, only 80 percent could be achieved in practice in the individual mills.[7] In view of the varying rate of intensity of the *zafra* (sugar campaign)—at the beginning and at the end of the harvesting season only fractions of the overall capacity are being used—the overall average utilization is even lower, around 63 percent in my opinion, a figure that varies with the length of the harvest.[8] To deal with an empirical value, if 347,000 tons of cane could be processed daily in the existing plants, the required 45 million tons of the base year could be processed within 130 actual work or harvest days.[9]

Once we have established the daily harvest performance, we can calculate the number of workers needed in the field. Given the production technique used, the daily output of a harvester averaged 1.522 tons of sugar cane, an empirical figure from the postrevolutionary period that can be considered valid until 1969.[10] It can be assumed that for a daily harvest of 347,000 tons of cane, an average of 225,000 agricultural workers was needed.[11] Of these, two-thirds would be engaged in cutting cane while the others would clean the cane, load it, and transport it to the mill.

The capacity of the transportation system, which does not appear here as a variable of the production plan, had to be adequate for the sugar industry. Since sugar cane cannot be stored, but must be processed within twenty-four hours at the most, transportation time had to be kept to a minimum.

In order to evaluate the base data of the production plan mentioned so far, a short comparison with the prerevolutionary era is in order. The cultivated area needed in 1964 corresponds to the agricultural area reserved for the culture of sugar cane in the 1950s. Immediately after the revolution, land had been assigned to new crops at the expense of the sugar economy, some of which now had to be plowed up again. It is true that the projected yield of 45 tons per hectare had been reached before the revolution as peak yield, but after 1960 the yield was as much as 25 percent below the base figure. The decrease after the land reform was certainly due to organizational and climatic difficulties and, in theory at least, this yield could be corrected upward through appropriate measures. Nevertheless, in the light of the past, the base value seems overly optimistic. I estimate the industrial yield of the plan as approximately equivalent to the average results between 1951 and 1959, which, with proper maintenance of equipment, should be attainable without difficulty under the given circumstances.[12]

The existing industrial and transportation capacity had been sufficient between 1951 and 1959 for processing and conveying a daily average of 440,000 tons of sugar cane, which puts it at 20 percent above the anticipated figure. However, in 1964 the equipment was partly dilapidated because of the American embargo, so that repairs became a precondition for the success of the plan.

The 130-day harvest period was rather long as compared with earlier times. In the prerevolutionary time span we have examined, about 100 working days had been sufficient to harvest and process the same quantity of cane. However, the proposed extension had the advantage of reducing the demand for manpower (only 225,000 instead of 350,000 workers) and of lessening the seasonal character of the *zafra*. At the same time, lighter demands were made on the equipment, a desirable secondary effect in view of the spare-parts problem.

However, with regard to average work performance, there was a considerable discrepancy between the base value and actual results. Before the revolution, this average came to 1.335 tons per harvester, 15 percent lower than assumed. We have to keep in mind, however, that an ex post facto value has been postulated as the base quantity (until 1969). This could account for a discrepancy of this magnitude after capital goods were substituted for manual labor on a large scale, especially in cleaning and loading cane in the field. It does seem rather high as a base value for the production plan, but it will be retained as a constant parameter for the whole planning period.[13]

On the whole it would appear that the base data of the production variables used are within the realm of possibility and that, therefore, the Cubans proceeded from a realistic evaluation of the performance capacity of the sugar economy. How, then, were the variables to be modified in order to reach a production of 10 million tons of raw sugar?

The sugar plan projected a gradual production increase to 78 percent above the base value by 1970 (see table 13). This required a rise of 87 percent in cane production to 84 million tons. Consequently—if we apply the law of diminishing marginal returns to the sugar economy—the industrial extraction rate had to drop to 12 percent. The required record harvest anticipated a 50 percent extension of the cultivated area to 1.5 million hectares, and to compensate for this proportionately insufficient increase, the agricultural yield had to be improved. An increase of 24 percent to 56 tons was scheduled.[14]

In the industrial sector, the plan called for a 22 percent expansion of production capacity to 670,000 tons. If we assume the utilization parameter to be constant at 63 percent, 420,000 tons of cane would now be processed daily, which corresponds to a performance increase of 22 percent. The harvest of 84 million tons could be completed in about 200 days, which meant lengthening the harvest season by 54 percent, concentrated in the first six months of 1970.[15]

The increase in the average number of workers needed during this period can also be estimated at 22 percent, provided the labor productivity parameter of 1.552 tons per day remained unchanged. Thus a seasonal mobilization of 280,000 harvest workers could be expected, two-thirds of them being *macheteros* (cutters). This last figure comes very close to Castro's statement of 1969, "that 200,000 men, working eight hours . . . [will] cut the cane needed for the 10 million ton *zafra*."[16]

This defines the individual objectives of the production plan until 1970. We must now deduce from the base data (1964) and the assigned goals (1970) the values of the individual variables for the intervening years of the plan. This requires a series of assumptions, because only the yearly production goal of raw sugar was officially known.

Assumption 1:   The industrial yield decreases by 0.1 percent of weight for each additional million tons of sugar produced. This assumption is in line with the base value and plan objective. It can also be substantiated in the following way: To increase the cane supply, it became necessary to cut cane before and after the optimum degree of maturity; extending the cultivated area increased transportation time to the processing plants; and less and less suitable land was available. All these factors reduced the sucrose content of the cane and, consequently, the industrial yield.

Assumption 2:   Agricultural yield increases in proportion to the rise in sugar production. This assumption is not based on any intrinsic law; its only object is to extrapolate the yearly increases within the framework of base values and target values. The implementation time lag of the required measures has to be taken into account in the early stages.

On the basis of assumptions 1 and 2, and knowing the yearly production goals for raw sugar, we can deduce the data for cane production and cultivated areas.

Assumption 3:   Plant capacity grows in proportion to the increase of cane production. Here too the only objective is to find as realistic a rate of increase as possible within the given framework. Again, at the start of the planning period the investment time lag has to be taken into account.

Assumption 4:   Current capacity utilization averages 63 percent. The utilization parameter is considered constant for the simple reason that no computation basis for differentiation exists. It may be argued that through organizational and technical rationalization utilization of individual mills could be improved, but this trend would be offset by the decreasing utilization of total capacity owing to the extension of the campaign.

Assumption 5: The current daily average performance per worker amounts to 1.522 tons of sugar cane. A change in the productivity of labor is equivalent in principle to a change in the substitution relationship between labor and capital. As will be shown in detail later, labor-saving investments were planned, especially in the preparation of land for cultivation, as well as in the cleaning and loading of sugar cane. If rationalization had been the only objective of the sugar plan, and not a larger sugar harvest, intensive capital investments could have increased labor productivity. However, the planned massive increase of production required such large expenditures of capital that though the present labor intensity of production could be expected to be maintained, it could hardly be decreased; that is, the production functions themselves would hardly change at all. As will be seen later, the projected investment activity was focused mainly on expanding plant capacity and increasing agricultural yield, not on labor substitution.[17] Any labor substitution that was accomplished probably would be counteracted by the fact that qualified harvesters were leaving in increasing numbers and had to be replaced by less-skilled workers. These considerations explain why the empirical value of 1.522 tons can be used as a constant parameter for the entire duration of the plan.

Taking into account assumptions 3, 4, and 5, we can now extrapolate the yearly planning data for plant capacity, daily cane production, and manpower. The overall reconstructed plan is shown in table 13.

Quantity Planning Within the Marketing Frame. Actually, the marketing plan should precede the production plan, since production goals are derived from marketing potential. There is evidence of preliminary Cuban studies on the basic conditions of the world sugar market that might restrict the expansion potential of the export sector.[18] In addition to this research, a study published in 1962 by the FAO on the sugar economy in 1970 might have been helpful.[19] It inquires into the production, consumption, and net imports of the nonsocialist countries and has been used here to deduce the sales potential of Cuban sugar on the free international market. It is followed by an ex post facto study attempting to determine the net import potential of the socialist world until 1970.

To ascertain the desired quantities for 1970, the FAO study used a projection of the production- and consumption-determining vari-

TABLE 13. The Production Plan (Quantity)

Variables	Base Year		1965		1966	
	Quant.	Index	Quant.	Index	Quant.	Index
Raw sugar, 1,000 t	5,625	100	6,000	107	6,500	116
Industrial yield, %	12.5	100	12.4	99	12.4	99
Sugar cane, 10^6 t	45	100	49	109	53	118
Agricultural yield, t/ha	45	100	45	100	47	104
Crop land, 1,000 ha	1,000	100	1,090	109	1,130	113
Capacity, 1,000 t	550	100	550	100	565	103
Utilization, %	63	100	63	100	63	100
Processed daily, 1,000 t	347	100	347	100	356	103
Harvest, days	130	100	141	108	149	115
Productivity of labor, t/day/W[a]	1.522	100	1.522	100	1.522	100
Workers, 1,000	225	100	225	100	234	103

a. Sugar cane harvest workers, of whom two-thirds are *macheteros*.

ables mentioned in chapter 1. In addition, a number of assumptions were made. In particular, the determination of production offered some problems and thus introduced an element of uncertainty, since it was not possible to forecast the future agricultural policy decisions of the producer countries. For instance, Cuba's intention to produce 10 million tons was not yet known. However, recent development trends had shown that all continents had registered a high growth rate of sugar production. Because of its advanced production techniques and shortage of agricultural land, slower growth could be expected in zone 1 (sugar beets) than in zone 3 (sugar cane), which still offered development potential.

The projection of demand relied primarily on future increases in income and population; for obvious reasons, the price of sugar as a determining variable was kept constant.

Production and consumption of individual countries were not assessed separately. The decisive fact here was that, especially in low-income countries where the backlog margin for increased consumption is highest, consumption is restricted to domestic production because of a chronic shortage of foreign exchange.

TABLE 13 (Continued)

1967		1968		1969		1970	
Quant.	Index	Quant.	Index	Quant.	Index	Quant.	Index
7,500	133	8,000	142	9,000	160	10,000	178
12.3	98	12.2	98	12.1	97	12.0	96
61	136	66	147	75	169	84	187
49	109	51	113	53	118	56	124
1,250	125	1,300	130	1,420	142	1,500	150
595	108	610	111	640	116	670	122
63	100	63	100	63	100	63	100
375	108	384	111	403	116	420	122
163	125	172	132	186	143	200	154
1.522	100	1.522	100	1.522	100	1.522	100
246	108	252	111	265	116	280	122

"The priority given to imports of capital equipment required for industrialization programs has been and will continue to be a major obstacle to the expansion of agricultural imports of low-income countries."[20] Only a slight stimulus in demand on the world sugar market could be expected from the countries of zone 3, which had a balanced sugar budget.

The study produced the following results: Net imports of zones 1 and 3 for 1970 (after deduction of all intrazonal trade exchanges) were estimated at just over 12 million tons; all in all, an increase of about 1 million tons over the 1957–59 position was anticipated (see table 14). Of the total quantity, 80 percent represented the demand of zone 1 alone which, however, only needed 750,000 additional tons. These would go almost exclusively to Japan, which has a substantial consumption backlog without foreign exchange problems, but where conditions for self-sufficiency were unfavorable. It is true that a substantial increase of net imports was anticipated for North America, but considering the sugar policy of the EEC, this would be offset by the development of the West European countries. Only the members of the European Free Trade Asso-

TABLE 14. Projection of Net Sugar Imports, for 1970
(1,000 m.t., raw value)

| Region | 1957–59 | | 1969–71 | | | |
	Quant.	Index	Low	Index	High	Index
Zone 1						
North America[a]	4,931	100	5,450	110	5,450	110
Western Europe	3,179	100	2,700	85	2,700	85
Japan	1,191	100	1,850	155	1,950	164
Subtotal	9,301	100	10,000	108	10,100	108
Zone 3						
Near East	811	100	1,000	123	1,200	148
North Africa	679	100	600	90	700	103
Rest of Africa[b]	329	100	500	152	660	200
Subtotal	1,819	100	2,100	115	2,560	141
Total	11,120	100	12,100	109	12,660	114

Source: FAO, "Agricultural Commodities Projections for 1970," Special Supplement to *FAO Commodity Review 1962* (Rome, 1962), pt. II, p. 36.
a. Including Puerto Rico and Hawaii.
b. Excluding South Africa, Mauritius, and Réunion.

ciation (EFTA) could be counted as net importers. In addition, the main potential markets for the sale of Cuban sugar were the Near East and North Africa, where import demand depended greatly on progress by ongoing development programs for local sugar economies.

On that basis it was not possible to quantify exactly the demand on the free sugar market, since the sugar budgets of the individual countries (and not of the zones) remained relevant in this context, as did the trading volume within the closed markets. Therefore, the FAO was able only to estimate roughly that Cuba could sell 2 million tons on the free international market until 1970, assuming that world market prices would remain constant.[21] This projection proved correct. In 1968, when a new sugar agreement was worked out, Cuba's export quota was set at slightly above 2 million tons (approximately 10 million tons were allocated); in fact, Cuba sold almost exactly 2 million tons in 1970.[22]

If we accept this figure as the basic indicator of sales in the free market in 1970, the additional assumption may be made that the Cuban planners expected to sell 1.75 million tons a year until 1969—as much as the average sales during the first years after the revolution—and thereafter increase sales by 250,000 tons a year. Thus, the potential for expansion of sugar exports on the free international market was limited. The crucial question then arose whether the socialist countries would be in a position to import substantially larger quantities of sugar from Cuba.

"Whether by 1970 the net imports of the Sino-Soviet area will be nil or as high as 4 or 5 million tons is largely a question of policy."[23] In these words the FAO declined to include the socialist countries in its projections. Nevertheless, the state of the sugar trade in zone 2 is of fundamental interest to us.

Basically, the socialist countries were geared to a balanced sugar budget, that is, autonomy within their zone. In 1960, the Soviet Union started importing larger quantities of Cuban sugar and absorbed the surplus mostly by raising domestic consumption. If Cuba wanted to exceed the 3 million tons of sugar sold eventually in the socialist camp, then China was really the natural trading partner because of its population and its potentially higher consumer demand. There, an increase of per capita consumption of only one kilo would have produced an additional demand of half a million tons or more.[24]

Instead of an FAO-style projection, I shall construct in table 15 a production forecast for zone 2 from ex post facto data, assuming that the actual figures for 1970 correspond to the target figures at

TABLE 15. Ex Post Facto Projection of Net Sugar Imports, Zone 2, 1970
(1,000 m.t., raw value)

Country	Production (1,000 t)	Population (1,000)	Per Capita Consumption (kg)	Total Consumption (1,000 t)	Balance (1,000 t)
USSR	10,125	242,554			
Variant 1			37.2	9,023	1,102
2			42.5	10,304	179
3			47.8	11,594	−1,469
COMECON[a]	4,175	105,758			
Variant 1			29.6	3,130	1,045
2			34.2	3,618	557
3			38.8	4,103	72
China	2,250	847,700			
Variant 1			2.5	2,119	131
2			3.3	2,760	− 510
3			4.1	3,475	−1,225
Total	16,550	1,196,012			
Variant 1			11.9	14,272	2,278
2			13.9	16,682	− 132
3			16.0	19,172	−2,622

Sources: Computed from data in FAO, Agricultural Commodities Projections 1970–1980 (Rome, 1971), vol. 2, p. 7; and Hawaiian Sugar Planter's Association, Sugar Manual 1972 (Honolulu, 1972), pp. 36–37.
a. Excluding USSR, including Yugoslavia.

the beginning of the five-year plans in 1965. For the consumption forecast, three variants have been selected:

Variant 1: Per capita consumption until 1970 remains frozen at the 1965 level (pessimistic variant).

Variant 2: Per capita consumption is equivalent to the actual situation in 1970 (probable variant).

Variant 3: Per capita consumption until 1970 is being raised by the difference between variants 1 and 2 (optimistic variant).

The difference between production and consumption is identical to the net trade volume; if the balance is negative, it is equivalent to net imports, for which there also exist three variants.

Obviously, this type of ex post facto analysis has only hypothetical value. Nevertheless, the results are informative: If the countries of zone 2 had increased their total consumption of sugar on the basis of population growth alone, they would have become net exporters on a much larger scale. This alternative was definitely in the realm of possibility, since in 1965 individual consumption (excluding China), even without additional imports from Cuba, had almost reached the level of the EEC countries.

Variant 2 shows that only China could not satisfy its actual consumption through its own production. The deficit was made up, however, by the surplus of the COMECON countries (excluding the Soviet Union), whereas the USSR itself had a balanced sugar budget.

Only in variant 3 would the Soviet Union also have shown a substantial deficit—though with a per capita consumption on the same level as that of the United States—while the COMECON countries (excluding the USSR) would have been just about self-sufficient. On the whole, the net import capacity of the socialist countries under the stated assumptions would have increased by 1970 to about 2.5 million tons, which, added to the free-market figure, means that Cuba could have exported a maximum of 5 million tons of sugar—approximately the same amount as before the revolution.

In conclusion, an increase in Cuban sugar sales was not a necessity for the socialist countries. But the Soviet Union in particular had reasons going beyond considerations of balanced sugar budgets. It was important to them that Cuba be in a position to balance its trade deficit through additional exports. The decisive factor for an increase of Cuba's export quota beyond Soviet sugar needs was a political decision of the USSR to protect the development of the first socialist country in Latin America through continued material support.

How could the Soviet Union absorb additional Cuban exports? Theoretically, restricting Soviet production would have been the most economically sound solution for both sides. However, this would have made the sugar supply of the Soviet population dependent on the success of the Cuban sugar plan. Even in case of failure, Cuba would have been forced to adhere strictly to its contracts with the USSR, but at the expense of the international free market on whose currency revenue the Cuban economy depended as much as ever. Furthermore, since the Soviet Union's sugar beet expansion program was already underway, a temporary cutback at this point would have made little sense.

In view of the existing level of Soviet consumption, the only possible increase would be in marginal sectors; the additional importation of even 1 million tons would increase individual consumption by four kilograms. The only remaining practical solution was thus to offset at least part of the new sugar imports from Cuba with stepped-up Soviet exports. However, even though the Soviet Union was offering refined sugar only, its exports would compete indirectly with Cuban exports on the free international market and thus would have a tendency to depress prices. Such a solution was acceptable from the Cuban point of view only if the USSR were to make up the potential loss by paying an agreed subsidized price for Cuban sugar. At the same time, part of these imports had to be paid in foreign exchange to compensate for the indirect transfer of hard currency—approximately 15 percent of

Cuban sugar costs go for inputs imported from the West.

In January 1964 Fidel Castro visited Moscow. He returned with a trade agreement between Cuba and the Soviet Union calling for deliveries of a total of 24 million tons of sugar between 1965 and 1970. The agreed price was 6.11¢ per pound, which was above the average world market price of the past years.[25] Agreements were also signed with the other socialist countries, but no exact information as to their terms is available. However, they had no reason not to extend to Cuba the same terms as the Soviet Union. As far as the yearly sales volume is concerned, Castro's 1964 statement according to which the sugar harvest of 1970 was already sold will be used here as the point of departure.[26] Taking into account estimated domestic consumption and sales on the free market as well as to the USSR, it may be assumed that the other COMECON members, including China and Yugoslavia, were prepared to absorb whatever balance remained, which in 1970 amounted to roughly 2 million tons.

At this point it has to be borne in mind that official planning data are available only with respect to Cuban production and to Cuban sales to the Soviet Union. I estimated domestic consumption on the basis of the known fact that per capita sugar consumption in Cuba was one of the highest in the world, well above the "saturation" point of 50 kilograms. This was due in part to the fact that up to 1969 sugar was among the few nonrationed food items and was offered at a relatively low price, and in part to the fact that in Cuba the need for sweets was no longer satisfied by fruit, as is customary in other tropical countries.[27]

Estimated consumption, then, is another relatively reliable planning factor, together with total export volume, which can be determined by deducting domestic consumption from total production. However, we have to bear in mind that the respective percentages of sales on the free market and on the COMECON and China sugar market may have differed from the ratio assumed in the present analysis. (See table 16.)

I shall now attempt to evaluate the financial data of the sugar plan. However, this assessment is merely hypothetical since, in contrast to sugar quantity planning, little information of Cuban origin is available. A monetary assessment is attempted only because the explicit purpose of the sugar plan was to increase import capacity. Consequently, the planning of export earnings is of interest. Thereafter I shall address the question of the extent to which the sugar plan respected the principle of economic profitability, a question which raises the problem of computing production expenditures so that the juxtaposition of expenditures and earnings pertains only to the marketing of sugar abroad.

TABLE 16. The Marketing Plan (Quantity)
(1,000 m.t., raw value)

Countries	Base Year		1965		1966	
	Quant.	Index	Quant.	Index	Quant.	Index
Free market	1,600	100	1,750	110	1,750	110
Closed markets						
USSR	2,000	100	2,100	105	3,000	150
COMECON and						
China[a]	1,500	100	1,650	110	1,200	80
Subtotal	3,500	100	3,750	107	4,200	120
Total exports	5,100	100	5,500	108	5,950	117
Consumption	500	100	500	100	550	110
Production	5,600	100	6,000	107	6,500	116

a. All socialist countries other than the USSR.

Cost Structure of the Production Plan. The principal end product of sugar production is raw sugar. In addition, there are usable by-products, such as bagasse (sugar cane from which the juice has been extracted), which traditionally is the basic energy-producing fuel in the mill, and above all molasses, which can be used as feed or distilled into alcohol. The cultivation and industrial processing of sugar cane are the basic production elements of the end product. Therefore, the production and processing cost of the raw material will be used to compute the cost of raw sugar. As source material for Cuban sugar production we have Armando Betancourt's information for 1965.[28]

Using table 17, the average cost per ton of sugar cane produced and processed with a close to optimum production output[29] can be calculated.

In order to analyze this rough outline, an attempt will be made to reduce the data to a form borrowed from business cost accounting practices, according to which production expenditures are apportioned systematically to cost items and allocated to cost sectors. The result is the cost structure for producing and processing one ton of Cuban sugar cane that appears in table 18.

Even this simplified breakdown of the data by cost items and

TABLE 16 (Continued)

1967		1968		1969		1970	
Quant.	Index	Quant.	Index	Quant.	Index	Quant.	Index
1,750	110	1,750	110	2,000	125	2,250	141
4,000	200	5,000	250	5,000	250	5,000	250
1,150	77	600	40	1,300	87	2,000	133
5,150	147	5,600	160	6,300	180	7,000	200
6,900	135	7,350	144	8,300	163	9,250	181
600	120	650	130	700	140	750	150
7,500	133	8,000	142	9,000	160	10,000	178

cost sectors permits a formal critique. "Agriculture," "Transportation," and "Administration" cannot be apportioned to cost items; consequently, it is not possible to establish the respective percentages. The cost sector "Harvesting," however, is allocated in its entirety to direct labor costs. Hence, costs of materials and indirect wage costs (which cannot be negligible in socialist Cuba) are ignored. Again, for the "Industry" sector, only the insignificant costs of additional material inputs appear as total. Energy consumption is not taken into consideration; nor are labor costs, depreciation, and so forth. The obvious conclusion is that the given data are incomplete and therefore that the total average costs have been assessed at too low a level.

With these reservations in mind, I will try to derive raw sugar costs from sugar cane costs. With an industrial yield of 12.5 percent, 125 kilograms of raw sugar should be extracted from one ton of sugar cane. Thus, costs according to the above computations would amount to Cub$10.75, or barely 4¢ per pound. This conversion clearly shows the importance of the industrial yield in the average cost of raw sugar. If the extraction rate decreases, costs go up proportionately.

TABLE 17. Model for Cost Calculation

Sector	Costs (Cub$/t)
Agriculture	
Raw material	6.7699
Transportation	1.0325
Labor[a]	1.3665
Subtotal	9.1689
Industry	
Additional inputs	0.0921
Total direct costs	9.2610
Indirect costs[b]	1.4890
Total average costs	10.7500

a. Harvesting only. According to Betancourt, the estimated total payroll for a daily harvest of 425,000 tons was Cub$555,000 ("Study in Extraneous Matter in Sugar Cane," *CubaAzúcar* [September–December 1966]).

b. Administrative cost only, estimated by Betancourt, ibid.

Charging the total sugar cane costs to the raw sugar implies that no costs are allocated to the by-products. Hence, the raw sugar costs arrived at with this method may appear inordinately high. On the other hand, this compensates for the reservation made earlier that sugar cane costs have been assessed at too low a level.[30]

To compute the total cost of the projected yearly sugar production several additional assumptions have to be made:

Assumption 1: Factor costs remain constant. This assumption is unrealistic because costs must have fluctuated during the period covered by the plan. If the present computation of average costs is to be retained as a basis, such variations have to be excluded.

Assumption 2: The marginal costs of cane production and processing remain constant for the cost sectors "Agriculture," "Harvesting," "Transportation," and "Industry." Constant marginal costs, taking assumption 1 into consideration, presuppose a constant production function. Here, too, we have to disregard the fact that with increasing harvest mechanization,

TABLE 18. Structure of Average Costs for Produced and Processed Cuban Sugar Cane, 1965 (percentages)

Cost Items / Cost Sectors	Labor	Equipment	Indirect Costs	Total
Agriculture	—	—	—	62
Harvesting	13	—	—	13
Transportation	—	—	—	10
Industry	—	1	—	1
Administration	—	—	—	14
Total	—	—	—	100

improved yield per hectare, and so forth, the production function certainly could vary.

Assumption 3: "Administration" costs are fixed charges and thus decreasing average costs. Here again the reservation applies that this assumption does not quite conform to reality. In addition, this entails a restriction of assumption 2, according to which the relationship between factor input and the production and processing of sugar cane was to remain constant.

It would also seem reasonable to consider investments in the cost accounting. The total amount of investments for the duration of the plan was estimated in 1965 at Cub$1.020 billion,[31] and while this figure was later reduced, the initial amount will be used here.

The amortization of new investments thus appears as a further cost item.

To determine the yearly depreciation, two factors must be determined: the investment allocation schedule, and the depreciation rate. With the help of the total projected investments, sugar cane production and processing by 1970 was to have increased by 39 million tons, an average investment outlay of Cub$26.15 per ton. By assuming—in the absence of more reliable information—

TABLE 19. The Production Plan (Financial)

Variables	Base Year		1965		1966	
	Quant.	Index	Quant.	Index	Quant.	Index
Sugar cane						
Production, 1,000 t	45,000	100	49,000	109	53,000	118
Increase, 1,000 t	—	—	4,000	100	4,000	100
Investments, 10^6	105	100	105	100	209	200
Cane costs						
Administration, 10^6	67	100	67	100	67	100
Variable costs, 10^6	417	100	454	109	491	118
Depreciation, 10^6	—	—	5	100	10	200
Total costs, 10^6	484	100	526	109	568	117
Average costs/t, $	10.75	100	10.74	100	10.72	100
Raw sugar						
Production, 1,000 t	5,600	100	6,000	107	6,500	116
Industrial yield, %	12.5	100	12.4	99	12.4	99
Average cost/t, $	86.04	100	87.67	102	87.38	102
Average cost/lb., ¢	3.90	100	3.97	102	3.96	102

that this investment coefficient remains constant, the total investment volume can be prorated over the planning period according to the expansion of sugar cane cultivation. We must keep in mind, however, that there is a time lag of one year between the actual investment and its effect, so that the first investment had to be made as early as 1964, the base year, and the last in 1969; whereas amortization should be charged to production only in the output year. The depreciation rate, which is not uniform because of the differing useful lives of the means of production, will be set at 5 percent for accounting purposes, in line with the international pragmatic value for raw-sugar economies. A further assumption is that a linear depreciation method is used, that is, every year 5 percent of the total investments of the previous year will be charged to production costs.

With the general reservation that a model with a very limited empirical foundation has been used, the cost plan of Cuban sugar production until 1970 can now be reconstructed (table 19). The

TABLE 19 (Continued)

1967		1968		1969		1970	
Quant.	Index	Quant.	Index	Quant.	Index	Quant.	Index
61,000	136	66,000	147	75,000	169	84,000	187
8,000	200	5,000	125	9,000	225	9,000	225
131	125	235	224	235	224	—	—
67	100	67	100	67	100	67	100
565	135	611	147	695	167	778	187
21	420	28	560	39	780	51	1,020
653	135	706	146	801	165	896	185
10.70	100	10.69	100	10.68	100	10.67	100
7,500	133	8,000	143	9,000	160	10,000	178
12.3	98	12.2	97	12.1	96	12.0	96
87.07	101	88.25	103	89.00	103	89.60	104
3.95	101	4.00	102	4.03	103	4.06	104

point of departure is the production (and processing) of sugar cane, which serves as the basis for computing variable costs (Cub$9.2610 per ton). Administrative costs are kept constant at Cub$67 million. Taking depreciation into account, total production costs are then calculated. The result shows that the average costs for sugar cane remain constant for all practical purposes, because the diminishing fixed-cost percentage is offset by mounting depreciation. Therefore, the average costs of raw sugar are modified only by the industrial yield. Since the latter was to de-

·crease by 4 percent by 1970, the average costs increase accordingly.

The Marketing Plan's Financial Yield Structure. Cuba's
financial sugar revenue is composed of domestic consumption at
domestic price levels; of exports to the markets of the socialist
world at preferential prices; and of sales on the free market at
world market prices. The variations in inventory calculated at
clearing prices for accounting purposes ultimately serve as a
corrective factor. Since we are concerned mainly with export
production, domestic sugar revenue and variations in inventory
will be disregarded.

In accordance with the economic agreements concluded with
the socialist countries, the export revenues of Cuban sugar were to
be derived primarily from that market. As regards pricing, one may
start from the premise that the Soviet Union operated on the basis
of a clearing price of 6.11¢ per pound, or roughly $135 per ton, of
raw sugar. No standard prices are known for any of the other
socialist countries, but we may assume that these approximated
the one set by the USSR since, with the exception of China,
practically all COMECON countries had to compensate the Cuban
imports by their own exports, thereby depressing the sugar price
on the world market.

By analogy to the FAO projections, a constant price will be
assumed for the free international sugar market, for which forecasts regarding price evolution became particularly unreliable after the breakdown of the Sugar Agreement of 1958. Hereinafter
this price will be assumed equal to the lowest standard price
suggested in the Sugar Agreement of 1958, amounting to 3.25¢ per
pound, or just under $72 per ton. Though the average sugar price in
1963 climbed to 8.48¢ per pound,[32] this fluctuation is to be under-
stood also in the light of the dramatic drop in Cuban exports during
that year. It therefore constituted an exception.

On the basis of the assumed constant price, the export revenues
for the three separate markets can be calculated by means of the
known, quantity-related sales figures. The results are summarized
in table 20. As shown therein, the export revenue of Cub$600

million from the sales of raw sugar in the base year was to be increased to more than Cub$1 billion, to be ensured mainly through trade with the USSR.

Provided that the estimated production costs more or less conform to reality, the net revenues could be expected to grow at the same rate, since according to the computation at hand the rise in marginàl costs could be compensated by the growth of the marginal net revenue realized by the progressive shift of exports to the price-favorable socialist markets. Accordingly, the profit margin[33] may be expected to have fluctuated around 25 percent.

Finally, an important restriction must be added: The export revenues from the various separate markets cannot simply be added up to form a total. The socialist countries predominantly were to compensate their imports by shipments of their own goods, so the sugar price agreed upon constituted only one side of the terms of the exchange trade. Therefore, a truly meaningful analysis of import capability must be based on those reproduction costs for sugar which Cuba had to pay for its imports of goods from various countries. Such a computation will be attempted in connection with the study of the implementation of the plan but will not be anticipated while dealing with the planning phase.

The same objection also holds true where export revenues are being confronted by corresponding costs. I proceeded under the tacit understanding that the value of the Cuban peso was equal to that of the U.S. dollar.[34] Since a common currency denominator is needed in computing profitability, this fiction will be maintained for the time being. It will be explored further at a later point.[35]

If the present estimates agree to some extent with the Cuban planning values, the target figures generally can lay claim to economic soundness. It also becomes clear that the realization of the whole projection plan depended on the premise that sugar sales remained assured of a strong preferential sales market. The profit margin achieved in trading with socialist countries had to be broad enough to safeguard the profitability of sugar production, even when the price of sugar on the free international market fell below the break-even point.

Concurrently, the first danger signals appear: It is obvious that the realization of the sugar plan could not rest on Cuban output and production performance alone. To finance its vital imports, Cuba remained dependent on exports to the free international market

TABLE 20. The Marketing Plan (Financial)

Market	Base Year		1965		1966	
	Quant.	Index	Quant.	Index	Quant.	Index
Free market						
Sales volume, $10⁶	115	100	126	109	126	109
Price, ¢/lb.	3.25	100	3.25	100	3.25	100
Closed markets						
USSR						
Volume, $10⁶	270	100	283	105	405	150
Price, ¢/lb.	6.11	100	6.11	100	6.11	100
COMECON and China[a]						
Volume, $10⁶	202	100	223	110	162	80
Price, ¢/lb.	6.11	100	6.11	100	6.11	100
Subtotal						
Volume, $10⁶	472	100	506	107	567	120
Av. price, ¢/lb.	6.11	100	6.11	100	6.11	100
Total exports						
Revenues, $10⁶	587	100	632	108	693	118
Av. price, ¢/lb.	5.22	100	5.21	100	5.28	101
Total costs						
Exports, $10⁶	439	100	482	110	520	118
Average costs, ¢/lb.	3.90	100	3.97	102	3.96	102
Net revenues, $10⁶	148	100	150	101	173	116
Profit margin, %[b]	25.2	100	23.7	94	25.0	99

a. All socialist countries except the USSR.
b. Net revenues in percentage of export revenues.

within the frame of its planned projections. As long as no price-regulating sugar agreement was in force, a drop of only 0.5¢ per pound—a possibility to be taken very seriously—would entail for Cuba a loss in foreign currency of some $19 to 25 million which could only be compensated by additional exports of from 313,000 to 412,000 tons of sugar.[36] If such exports were to be reallocated at the expense of the socialist world markets, the resulting loss would rise automatically to $45 million without any change in the total volume of Cuban exports. Thus, any shift in the respective shares of the export market in favor of the free international market was

TABLE 20 (Continued)

1967		1968		1969		1970	
Quant.	Index	Quant.	Index	Quant.	Index	Quant.	Index
126	109	126	109	143	125	161	143
3.25	100	3.25	100	3.25	100	3.25	100
540	200	674	250	674	250	674	250
6.11	100	6.11	100	6.11	100	6.11	100
155	77	88	40	175	87	270	133
6.11	100	6.11	100	6.11	100	6.11	100
695	147	755	160	849	180	944	200
6.11	100	6.11	100	6.11	100	6.11	100
821	140	881	150	992	169	1,105	188
5.39	103	5.43	104	5.42	104	5.41	104
601	137	647	147	739	168	829	189
3.95	101	3.99	102	4.03	103	4.06	104
220	149	234	158	254	172	276	186
26.8	106	26.6	106	28.8	114	25.0	100

bound to have an adverse effect on Cuban import capability.

Such a reduction would also occur whenever the production goals could not be fulfilled. Such shortfalls, for reasons mentioned previously, would be entirely at the expense of the more favorably priced closed markets. Therefore, any drop of 1 million tons of raw sugar from the production goal would entail a cut in the export revenue of $135 million and at the same time—introducing an

altogether different dimension—a reduction of the national income
by 3 to 4 percent.

If in order to prevent such an occurrence every possible effort
were made to fulfill the production goal, for instance by extension
of the harvest time or intensification of the harvesting effort (always assuming a sufficient crop supply), marginal costs obviously
would rise sharply and simultaneously. As will be documented
more thoroughly for 1970, almost all short-term efforts to increase
production in the sugar economy have to be paid for by a loss in
industrial yield. If the latter dropped by 1 percent in weight from a
projected level of 10 million tons, the production costs, according
to the data at hand, would rise by a total of Cub$90 million.

If all three of these contingencies coincided, the danger was
great indeed that Cuba's development strategy would lead to an
economic setback. The Cuban leadership had sole responsibility
for fulfilling the production—if not the marketing—plan in its
financial and quantitative aspects. Therefore, a set of specific
measures was issued to insure the execution of the primary planning goals.

Measures for Realization of Proposed Goals

Originally, an investment of Cub$1 billion was deemed neces-
sary for the realization of the sugar plan.[37] The allocation of this
sum and the means by which it was to be made available form the
subject of this section.

Of the total planned investments, 45 percent were to be allocated
to the agricultural sector, 17 percent to processing the cane, 23
percent to the land and water transportation system, and the
remaining 15 percent to satellite industries (see table 21).

In the sector of sugar cane cultivation, attention was focused on
intensified soil exploitation in order to increase the yield per hectare. A substantial improvement in the agricultural yield seemed
all the more urgent since additional arable land could only be
allocated at the expense of other crops. This increase, then, was
promoted by a series of reciprocally complementary measures.

First, 70 percent of all available cane area was to be newly

TABLE 21. The Investment Plan
(in millions of Cuban pesos)

	Totals		Procurement							
			Domestic Economy		Total		Foreign Trade			
							Socialist Countries Only		Capitalist Countries Only	
Allocations	Amounts	%	Amounts	%	Amounts	%	Amounts	%	Amounts	%
Agriculture	465	45	205	52	260	42	253	53	7	5
Industry	170	17	80	20	90	14	65	13	25	17
Satellite industries	150	15	30	8	120	19	45	9	75	50
Land transportation	190	19	50	14	140	22	100	21	40	27
Water transportation	45	4	25	6	20	3	18	4	2	1
Totals	1,020	100	390	100	630	100	481	100	149	100
%	100	—	38	—	62	—	47	—	15	—

Source: Compiled from Michel Gutelman, *L'Agriculture socialisée à Cuba* (Paris, 1967), pp. 204–06.

planted so as to reduce the proportion of stubble cane (with diminishing agricultural and industrial marginal yields) in the overall harvest.[38] This meant that more than 1 million hectares had to be plowed up and prepared for the cultivation of sugar cane, half of it newly cleared soil and the rest cultivated land with low yields. Chronologically, this measure had to be granted first priority, since newly planted cane in Cuba requires an average of twelve months to reach maximum maturity. In order to fulfill the target figures for 1970, the new plantings had to be completed no later than the end of 1968. At the same time, this massive expansion program was to allow for the introduction on a large scale of higher-quality cane varieties.

Second, 20 percent of all cane area required for the 1970 harvest was to be equipped with irrigation canals.[39] Irrigation installations have become essential in modern sugar cane cultivation. They allow for a neutralization of climatic fluctuations and are a prerequisite for mechanizing the harvesting operation—though the latter has yet to become an accomplished fact in Cuba. The required expansion of the infrastructure, such as the installation of pumping stations, the development of water resources, and so forth, undoubtedly called for very large investments, but unfortunately no specific data are available regarding their magnitude.

Third, the use of fertilizers was to be intensified, and the fertilizer production capacity was to be expanded from 420,000 to 2 million tons.[40] Although the fertilizer program was scheduled for agriculture as a whole, the lead sector was to benefit most from the capacity expansion, since modern cane culture is inconceivable without massive applications of growth-stimulating and disease-inhibiting chemical preparations.

The agricultural sector of sugar production called not only for measures designed to promote more efficient soil utilization but also for labor-saving measures, particularly with regard to the cane harvest itself. Castro repeatedly characterized manual cane-cutting as slave labor.

It has often been argued that to reach production of 10 million tons of raw sugar (over 80 million tons of cane), Cuba first would have had to mechanize the harvesting operation totally. But a closer examination of the conditions for mechanization reveals that such a goal would have been rather unrealistic. That total mechanization of harvesting is indeed possible has been demonstrated convincingly by the Hawaiian sugar companies under soil conditions which, in part, were less favorable than those in Cuba, where experiments toward that same end had been going on for years. By 1958, technology had progressed to a point in Hawaii where only 1.80 man-hours were required to harvest one ton of sugar cane, while in Cuba the same operation still required 6 or more man-hours.[41] The capital-output ratio in Hawaii (calculated on the basis of harvesting machines, means of transportation, and energy) fluctuated at that time around 0.16, which corresponded to a capital input of approximately $20 per ton of raw sugar.[42] However, to approximate hypothetically the costs of a corresponding mechanization of the Cuban sugar harvest one cannot simply transpose this capital-output ratio without reservations, since the harvest in Cuba in 1958 lasted merely four months, while the Hawaiian harvest could be carried on throughout the year. Thus, in Cuba, the equipment utilization rate could only be one-third of that possible in Hawaii over a one-year period and, therefore, the capital-output ratio would have to be tripled. If one assumes a conservative ratio of only 0.45 (instead of 0.48), the capital investment for the mechanization of field labor would have amounted to over $56 per ton to achieve the same labor productivity as that recorded in Hawaii. According to the economic development plan ending in 1970, 10 million tons of raw sugar at a yearly capacity utilization rate of 63 percent would have required a capital-output ratio of 0.25, or roughly $30 per ton at 1957 prices, that is, a total capital investment of more than $300 million. If in addition one takes into account the upward price evolution for capital goods up to 1965, this amount would be considerably higher still.

Mechanization of the sugar harvest is only feasible and economically justifiable if the soil is cultivated intensively, for mechanical harvesting results in a loss of quality in the cane and in an increase in impurities which have to be washed out during extraction. The price exacted by both these drawbacks is a reduced industrial yield; the concomitant opportunity costs of a decreasing extraction rate were mentioned earlier.

Even though these hypothetical elaborations can indicate only broadly the implications inherent in the mechanization of the harvesting process, it is safe to conclude that it can only be deemed economical if the means of production are used throughout the year. But in such a case the preparation and processing of the cane require a number of additional corollary investments in both the agricultural and industrial sectors, the scope of which need not be examined here.

Thus, the Cubans, realizing that total mechanization of the harvest was out of the question for the time being, contented themselves with only a partial program by substituting machines for at least some of the manual operations. In this connection one Cuban innovation, the *centro de acopio*, was to prove its worth. This consists of equipment which cleans the cane already in the field and then loads it mechanically. By 1970, 400 such *centros* were to be installed throughout the island,[43] and even though the cut cane had to be brought there by truck or ox cart, these centrally located plants prepared the cane automatically for processing in the mills and loaded it by conveyor onto the railroad cars, thus allowing for a better utilization of the rail network.

The daily capacity of a *centro* is stated as amounting to 1,000 tons of cane.[44] If one assumes arbitrarily a utilization rate of 80 percent during the harvest (the *centros* are not mobile and cannot be moved at random during harvest), it would have been possible theoretically to process a total of at least 300,000 tons of cane by 1970, that is, 70 percent of the average daily production, by means of these *centros*. An additional 4,500 mobile cranes with an average capacity of 80 tons were presumably sufficient to mechanize completely at least the loading of the cane by 1970.

The laborious cutting operation remained substantially unchanged, even though its mechanization would appear particularly pressing in view of the growing shortage of available manpower during the peak season. Therefore, harvesting combines from the Soviet Union were introduced in 1965 which cut the cane, removed the leaves and tips, chopped up the cane, and loaded it on a tandem trailer. However, these particular combines could be operated only under very restrictive topographical conditions and required level ground, cane growing at a certain angle and at carefully spaced intervals, and so forth. Given these preconditions, such a combine could harvest and prepare for the mill some 50 tons of cane per day (1965), thus accomplishing the work of 30 men. The sugar plan anticipated the use of 1,000 of these combines, which would have been able to handle 12 percent of the average daily cane production in 1970.[45] Apparently the natural conditions in Cuba did not permit a wider application, since one may safely assume that otherwise full mechanization would have seemed worthwhile to the Cuban leadership, despite the very substantial financial investment.

Extensive investments in replacements and new purchases were also necessary in the transportation sector, since the existing system had to be adapted to the daily peak capacity of industrial cane-processing. This meant that appropriate transportation means and routes had to be provided—not an easy task in view of the continuing American embargo. It was assumed that the record harvest of 1970 could be transported by means of 29,000 freight cars and 800 locomotives (of which 580 were overhauled steam locomotives), 17,000 trailers with 6,000 tractors and 5,500 trucks, and—as a relic of old times—19,000 ox carts. Of these, 2,000 freight cars, 85 diesel locomotives, 2,900 tractors, and 850 trucks were to be imported, while the remaining vehicles were to be supplied from existing stocks and renovated.[46]

The most important task was the overhaul of the railway system, which was to carry 80 percent of the cut cane from the *centros* to the proposed large-scale mills whose capacity would exceed the cane supply available in their immediate areas.

By 1970 over 9 million tons of sugar were to be exported, but to much more distant markets than before. In view of the less frequent sailings of the larger freighters, the warehouse and port facilities also had to be expanded. Therefore, the sugar plan foresaw the operation of four seaports capable of handling a total of 5 million tons of bulk sugar to be transported by rail from the mills in their vicinity, stored, and then loaded on the freighters by conveyor belts.[47] This new way of proceeding is unquestionably more economical than the traditional manner of expediting export goods, but it requires large investments. Four such ports were projected, and three of these were in operation by 1967, in Guajabal, Matanzas, and Cienfuegos.

In the industrial sector, a technical limit was imposed on daily cane production by the processing capacity of the sugar mills. In theory it should have been possible to handle the sugar production projected for 1970 with the existing installations, though only by extending the harvest period and suffering the consequent drop in marginal industrial yield. Thus, the more the processing capacity was to be expanded, the higher would be the industrial yield, since correspondingly larger quantities of cane could be processed at optimum maturity. However, in view of the labor-intensive harvesting process, an upper limit to the potential capacity expansion was set by the available manpower, whose average annual utilization was bound to decrease as the harvest period was shortened. The Cuban planners pegged the expansion of processing capacity midway between these two poles at 120,000 additional tons of cane per day. By 1970 Cuba was to have, as before, a total of 152 sugar mills, but by then these would be equipped with 182 tandem aggregates which allow for continuous processing without any stoppage for maintenance. Thirteen of these mills were to be expanded to a capacity of between 10,000 and 14,000 tons daily and together were to handle over one-fourth of the total daily production. But in view of prolonged neglect and deterioration, investments were concentrated mainly on renovation of the sugar plants. The government selected 113 mills in which either the production rhythm was to be accelerated through rationalization measures or capacity was to be increased by expanding existing installations. In making this selection, they used age and location of the mills as criteria.[48] All plants were examined with regard to their suitability

for expansion and continued operation, and the import requirements were then ascertained on the basis of the difference between
the old, operable installations and the total requirements in industrial material. This list of required imports included 7 tandem mills
with an overall capacity of 56,000 tons; the list of restorable old
equipment only included 3 tandem mills.[49] One may assume,
therefore, that an increase of capacity above 610,000 tons was to
be achieved in principle by increasing the processing speed in the
mills—a proposition which is bound to give some pause to the
outsider in view of the fact that the newest plant dated from 1925.[50]

The development of sugar satellite industries was to be given
priority only after 1970, in spite of the original capital outlay for
that purpose of 19 percent of total investments. It is obvious that
cuts had to be made in this sector for the time being. Nevertheless,
it was expected that by 1970 all preliminary steps for the operational readiness of the proposed ancillary industries would be
completed. In view of the limited domestic demand, here again the
emphasis was to be focused on export production, especially that
of refined sugar, molasses, alcohol, and yeast.

If capital formation is subdivided into the three component parts
of machines, installations, and labor, it becomes clear that in view
of Cuba's lack of capital-goods production, the first two components had to originate almost exclusively abroad. At most, Cuba
could provide old, reusable material, as well as, of course, the
required manpower. It is not surprising, therefore, that the import
component was estimated at over 60 percent of the proposed
overall investments (see table 21). Of these imports, 77 percent
were to originate in socialist countries; the balance, in the capitalist industrialized nations.

The import components according to allocation categories were
smaller for the sugar economy (agriculture and industry) than for
the corollary sectors of transportation and satellite industries (see
table 22), which means that capital formation in the cultivation and
processing of sugar cane was less dependent on the world market.
As regards the agricultural sector, it was significant also that 98
percent of the required capital goods could be supplied by socialist

countries, a fact which, in view of Cuba's long-term agreements with the latter, constituted an additional safety factor. However, the proportion of imports from the Western nations rose sharply for the sectors of industry, transportation, and satellite industries. At the same time the investment share of the domestic economy dropped to 32 percent in the transportation sector, and to 20 percent for satellite industries. Since capital goods from the Western world market had to be paid in foreign currencies which, in the main, had to be obtained through sugar sales, it became obvious that capital formation in the sugar economy could be influenced greatly by fluctuations of the sugar price on the world market.

In principle, the import of capital goods from socialist countries also had to be financed by Cuban sugar exports, but since the clearing price of 6.11¢ per pound agreed upon for these transactions deviated substantially from the assumed foreign currency price of 3.25¢ per pound for raw sugar on the free international market, table 21, which shows the investment volume at purchase costs, conveys a somewhat distorted picture. Only the cost of reproduction of the investments could be of real relevance to Cuba, and these costs were determined, in the case of imports, by the production costs of raw sugar to be traded on the various markets. Table 22 contains these supplemental data, which lead to the conclusion that, on the basis of a sugar price of $135 per ton, a total of 3,563,000 tons of raw sugar had to be exported to the socialist markets in order to pay for the purchase from these countries of capital goods valued at $481 million,[51] while for capital goods valued at $149 million, 2,085,000 tons of raw sugar at a price of $72 per ton were to be exported to the capitalist countries. By referring to the earlier cost computation for raw sugar, the hypothetical reproduction costs of the imported capital goods can now be calculated. Assuming average median costs of 4¢ per pound, or $88 per ton, the cost of production for capital goods originating in the socialist countries amounted to Cub$314 million, and for those originating in the capitalist countries to Cub$183 million. Thus, the import component, with a total of Cub$497 million, sank to 56 percent of the overall investments; but at the same time the com-

TABLE 22. The Financing Plan

	Allocations									
	Agriculture		Industry		Transportation		Satellite Industries		Totals	
Origin of Imports	Amounts	%	Amounts	%	Amounts	%	Amounts	%	Amounts	%
Investments at Procurement Costs (millions of Cuban pesos)										
Socialist countries	253	98	65	72	118	74	45	38	481	77
Capitalist countries	7	2	25	28	42	26	75	62	149	23
Total imports	260	100	90	100	160	100	120	100	630	100
Domestic economy	205	44	80	43	75	32	30	20	390	38
Imports	260	56	90	57	160	68	120	80	630	62
Total investments	465	100	170	100	235	100	150	100	1,020	100
Investments at Reproduction Costs (millions of Cuban pesos)[a]										
Socialist countries	165	95	43	58	77	60	29	24	314	63
Capitalist countries	9	5	31	42	51	40	92	76	183	37
Total imports	174	100	74	100	128	100	121	100	497	100
Domestic economy	205	54	80	52	75	37	30	20	390	44
Imports	174	46	74	48	128	63	121	80	497	56
Total investments	379	100	154	100	203	100	151	100	887	100

Sources: Investments at procurement costs, see table 21. The computation of the reproduction costs of the imports was based on an assumed sugar price of $72/t for the capitalist countries, and of $135/t for the socialist countries. For the Cuban sugar costs, the value of $88/t given in the 1968 plan (p. 61) was used.
a. Imports expressed in sugar costs.

ponent share of imports from Western nations had risen to 37 percent of total imports.

Consequently, whenever the sugar price dropped on the free international market, the percentage share of the Western nations in the overall import volume (although its total value remained the same) would shift at the expense of the share of the socialist markets unless the proposed investments in industry, transportation, and, more particularly, satellite industries were to be curtailed. The results will show that the plan's stated goals for the year 1970 were achieved only in the sector of agriculture.

CHAPTER THREE

Implementation of the Development Strategy

THIS CHAPTER deals with the practical implementation of, and the results achieved by, Cuban development strategy up to 1970. Regulatory policy measures are excluded from consideration, since deviations from the elaborations set forth earlier remained marginal. The central subject is the fulfillment of the prospective sugar plan and, in particular, the "Great *Zafra*" of 1970. The methodology introduced earlier will be used to distinguish between quantitative results and results in terms of value.

Since the sugar revenue from the various types of markets up to 1970 remained the overriding determinant of Cuba's import capability, the development of foreign trade will be analyzed. In addition, certain other determining variables for import capability will be examined, chiefly the terms of trade, as well as the potential financing of the Cuban national economy by third-party nations, although this exceeds somewhat the scope of a narrowly defined study of trading conditions.

To be sure, import capability was only one of the basic determinants in the formulation of Cuban economic activities in sectors other than that of sugar. In conclusion, therefore, an attempt will be made to show the effects of the sugar plan both on economic investment policies as a whole and on employment policies. This will provide the foundation for an analytical summary of the significance of sugar policy for the development of the entire Cuban economy up to 1970.

The Sugar Economy

In describing the further development of the Cuban sugar economy, we are confronted with the problem of valuation. In principle, an international comparison might provide a standard for such an assessment, but this presumably would lead to difficulties in the production sector. Production conditions differ widely from region to region, and there is no basis for comparison with regard to the marketing situation.

On the other hand, the achievements of the Cuban sugar economy may be assessed from a macroeconomic perspective: If the development of the lead sector of the economy was successful, then the foundations for a "forward thrust" were assured, since this entailed the near doubling of import capability which could then be used increasingly to procure capital goods with which to expand further the entire agroindustrial complex. However, for the success of the sugar plan it was essential also that Cuban production outside the sugar sector not suffer from the unilateral concentration on the expansion of sugar production. If, in particular, the rest of the agricultural production were to decline as a result, the increased import capability would have to be used chiefly to purchase consumer goods, thus thwarting the formation of capital.

Unfortunately, the effects of the sugar plan on import capability and on all other economic activities cannot be measured with any degree of accuracy, since they depend on a multiplicity of other variables. Therefore, any evaluation of the relevance of the sugar plan for the Cuban economy as a whole can constitute only a summary approximation.

Finally, the achievements of the sugar economy can be measured through its microeconomic objectives, thereby introducing the sugar plan itself as a criterion for evaluation. Thus, I shall examine to what extent its development until 1970 corresponded to the proposed Cuban objectives.

Chronologically, the *zafra* of 1964 does not fall within the planning period.[1] Heretofore it has been assumed that the base data of the sugar plan did indeed refer to that year, but the plan basis referred more accurately to the average capability of the sugar economy prior to the first impact of the measures designed to increase production. The 1964 *zafra*, therefore, was used merely to check the accuracy of the base data, so that it would be somewhat misleading in this connection to speak of "plan fulfillment." Consequently, in the following summary the *zafra* of 1964 will be dealt with separately from the actual plan years 1965 to 1970.

The Zafra *of 1964*

The base data of the sugar plan were to correspond to the capabilities of the Cuban sugar economy prior to 1965, and the *zafra* of 1964 was to be the touchstone of the validity of these indicators. However, a series of extreme conditions obtained during that year, in both the production and marketing sectors, so that the results were atypical and cannot be considered proof of planning errors.

The raw sugar production yielded the results shown in table 23. As shown, there was sufficient cane land for production of over 5 million tons of raw sugar. If the historically "normal" volume was not achieved, this can be attributed to low agricultural and industrial yields. The yield per hectare was 8 tons lower than the (rather optimistically estimated) norm. The extraction rate was the lowest in twenty years. While more than 170,000 hectares of cane land had been freshly planted in the fall of 1962 and during the following spring, so that at least 17 percent of the harvested land consisted of *cana planta*,[2] this favorable circumstance was offset by Hurricane Flora, which devastated the island with a violence seldom experienced in the past, causing extensive damage to the fields. As a result, only 37 million tons of cane could be cut. In view of the low agricultural yield, the Cubans were obliged to harvest as thoroughly and, therefore, as long as possible. How arduous the harvesting process must have been is illustrated by the daily average harvest volume of only 315,000 tons, which was even smaller than in the preceding year.

Under these conditions, the end result of 4.5 million tons had to be termed satisfactory: The Cubans, after all, thereby succeeded as early as 1964 in reversing the downward trend and in overcoming the low point in sugar production of the preceding year (3.8 million tons).

During the harvesting operation, the Cuban government followed a policy of secrecy, fearing that any publication of the harvesting results—showing higher figures than in 1963—could lead the capitalist countries to manipulate the sugar price, which had been exceedingly high in 1963. Castro stressed the prospective problem of a scarcity of harvest workers,[3] as many *macheteros* had migrated to the cities in the wake of the revolution, a migration that was still continuing.[4] If our assumptions regarding the produc-

TABLE 23. Fulfillment of 1964 Planning Norms

Variables		Results	Results as % of planning norms
S	(1,000 t)	4,475	80
i	(%)	12.03	96
C	(10^6 t)	37.2	83
a	(t/ha)	37	82
A	(1,000 ha)	1,002	100
P	(1,000 t)	550	100
p	(%)	57	90
c	(1,000 t)	316	91
H	(days)	118	91
l	(t/day/N)	1.522	100
N	(1,000)	208	92

Sources: S, i, c, H from JUCEPLAN, *Boletín Estadístico 1970* (Havana, n.d.), p. 136; *C, a, A* from ibid., p. 50; all shown for 1964–70. *P,* from H. Hirschmuller and H. J. Delavier, "Vor der grossen Zafra," in *Zeitschrift fur Zuckerindustrie,* 1969, installment 2, p. 4, is for 1964–69. $p = c \cdot 1,000/P$; l estimated by the author, assumed constant during plan period; $N = c/l$.

tivity of labor are correct, only some 200,000 harvest workers actually participated in the *zafra*. At the same time, Castro made clear that the superannuated industrial installations permitted little hope for improvements in the utilization of existing capacity. Thus, any increase in production could be achieved only by extending the harvest period. In addition to an increase in the agricultural yield to ensure a sufficient supply of cane, this in turn presupposed the planting of new cane varieties which would allow an intensification of the "little *zafra*."[5]

With regard to the export situation, Castro's report sounded optimistic.[6] The Cuban economy was in a position to market over 4 million tons of sugar on the international market. The results may be summarized as in table 24.[7]

It is to be noted first that domestic consumption in 1964 exceeded 400,000 tons, so that the export volume Cuba realized that year was made possible only by drawing on existing stocks.[8]

With regard to export allocations, the quantitative objectives for the free market and the Soviet Union were respected in the main. The remaining socialist countries played the role of a residual

TABLE 24. Fulfillment of 1964 Export Norms

Export Allocations	Sugar, Raw Value	
	1,000 t	% of proposed norm
Free market	1,526	95
USSR	1,937	97
COMECON and China[a]	714	48
Total exports	4,177	82
Domestic consumption and changes in inventory	299	60
Production	4,476	80

a. All socialist countries except the USSR.

market. That Cuba sold over 1.5 million tons of raw sugar on the free market in spite of relatively low sugar production was due to the favorable price situation. Even though the price fluctuated widely through the year, from a high of 11.18¢ per pound to a low of 2.53¢, the median price of 5.86¢ was nevertheless still well over Cuban production costs.[9] If Cuba actually obtained that price, this resulted in foreign exchange revenue of $200 million. Only speculative assumptions can be made with regard to the price conditions on the socialist markets. Applying the computation method suggested for the years 1965 to 1970 yields a median price of 6¢ per pound, so that one may assume that the fixed price negotiated with the USSR within the framework of the sugar forecast plan already was in effect the previous year in trade with all the socialist countries.

Parenthetically, in reporting on his trip to the Soviet Union, Castro asserted that the long-term preferential sugar price had not been set at the insistence of Cuba but actually constituted an offer by the USSR, irrespective of the fact that the socialist countries, after all, were not responsible for the price fluctuations on the free international market.[10] On the other hand, as I mentioned earlier, Cuba could lay an economically legitimate claim to a subsidized sugar price on the part of all COMECON countries.

TABLE 25. Implementation of the Quantity Production Plan

Variable	1965		1966	
	Quant.	%[a]	Quant.	%[a]
Raw sugar, 1,000 t	6,156	103	4,537	70
Industrial yield, %	12.15	98	12.32	99
Sugar cane, 10^6 t	50.7	103	36.8	70
Agricultural yield, t/ha	48	107	38	81
Cane land, 1,000 ha	1,055	97	979	87
Capacity, 1,000 t	550	100	550	97
Utilization, %	71	113	65	103
Daily processing, 1,000 t	390	112	361	101
Harvest period, days	130	92	102	68
Productivity, t/day/N[b]	1.522	100	1.522	100
Workers, 1,000	256	112	237	101

a. In percentage of plan objectives.
b. It will be assumed that the productivity of labor remained constant "accord-

In the light of this support, we can understand Castro's enthusiasm when he prophesied that Cuba would emerge victorious in a price war with the capitalist countries on the free international market: "And even if sugar should be quoted at two cents . . . even if it should be quoted at one cent, we shall see who emerges as the victor in this test of strength between the capitalist and the socialist production methods. . . . In five or six years this problem will be solved once and for all."[11] This was to be interpreted as meaning that by then Cuba, because of its more advantageous production costs, would have driven the other producing nations out of competition and would thus have a monopoly on the demand of the free international market.[12]

Implementation of the Sugar Plan from 1965 to 1970

Table 25 summarizes the performance of the quantitative production plan. The production target of 47 million tons of raw sugar could not be reached even approximately. In the six years of the plan, only 35 million tons were produced, averaging more or less the production in the last years before the revolution.

TABLE 25 (Continued)

1967		1968		1969		1970	
Quant.	%[a]	Quant.	%[a]	Quant.	%[a]	Quant.	%[a]
6,236	83	5,165	65	4,459	50	8,538	85
12.26	100	12.19	100	11.02	91	10.71	89
50.9	83	42.8	65	41.6	55	81.0	96
49	100	42	82	44	83	56	100
1,039	83	1,012	78	937	66	1,455	97
550	92	550	90	550	86	620	93
69	110	69	110	56	89	60	95
382	102	379	99	308	76	373	89
133	82	113	66	135	73	217	109
1.522	100	1.522	100	1.522	100	1.522	100
251	101	249	99	202	76	245	89

ing to plan." Under this assumption, the number of harvest workers can be ascertained.

The industrial yield remained satisfactory until 1968 chiefly because up to that point no substantial increase in production could be achieved. In connection with the record harvest of 1970, an alarming drop in that yield was noted.

Up to 1969 it proved impossible to produce sufficient cane to satisfy the processing capacity and, despite extensive efforts, here too production remained at prerevolutionary levels. Nevertheless, improvements were made in agricultural yield, particularly in 1970, so one may speak fairly of an intensification of cane cultivation.

In view of the sluggish cane production, the expansion of industrial capacity also was neglected; the existing installations were sufficient for the required processing. Only in 1969 and 1970 were serious efforts made to increase capacities, and these measures came too late. The poor management of the new facilities and the advanced age of the old ones were directly responsible for the drop in the extraction rate.

TABLE 26. Implementation of the Quantity Marketing Plan
(1,000 m.t., raw value)

Countries	1965		1966	
	Quant.	%[a]	Quant.	%[a]
Free markets	1,706	107	1,173	67
Japan alone	415	—	360	—
Closed markets				
USSR	2,456	117	1,820	60
COMECON and China[b]	1,154	70	1,442	117
China alone	398	—	620	—
Subtotal	3,610	96	3,262	78
Total exports	5,316	93	4,435	75
Domestic consumption[c] and changes in inventory	840		102	
Production	6,156		4,537	

a. In percentage of plan objectives.
b. All socialist countries outside the USSR.
c. Computed as the difference between production and total exports.

In comparison with the prerevolutionary period, the harvest season had been extended so that, on the one hand, the plants were not fully utilized, while on the other hand, the flattening out of the seasonal labor peaks reduced manpower requirements. If labor productivity remained constant—as is assumed in table 25—the harvests were brought in regularly with a total of barely a quarter-million field workers, much fewer than in earlier times.

Table 26 shows the implementation of the quantitative marketing plan. Between 1965 and 1970 Cuba exported just under 32 million tons of raw sugar and largely fulfilled the planned quotas for the nonsocialist and socialist markets, except the Soviet Union. Thus, the entire shortfall in production of 12 million tons reduced exports to the preferential market of the USSR, which paid the most favorable sugar price. As was to be expected, Japan gained increasing importance as a potential buyer of sugar on the free international market, while on the socialist market (excluding

TABLE 26 (Continued)

1967		1968		1969		1970	
Quant.	%ᵃ	Quant.	%ᵃ	Quant.	%ᵃ	Quant.	%ᵃ
1,758	100	1,418	81	1,924	96	2,104	94
542	—	555	—	1,018	—	1,221	—
2,473	62	1,831	37	1,352	27	3,105	62
1,452	126	1,364	227	1,523	117	1,697	85
556	—	431	—	445	—	530	—
3,925	76	3,195	57	2,875	46	4,802	69
5,683	82	4,613	63	4,799	58	6,906	75
553		552		−340		1,632	
6,236		5,165		4,459		8,538	

the USSR) China kept sugar purchases at a constant quantitative level, irrespective of its large percentage share in imports.

Table 27 summarizes the implementation of the cost scheduling plan. This is based on the assumption that the direct unit costs per ton of processed sugar cane remained constant at Cub$9.2610, which does not correspond to reality but was adopted for lack of more reliable data.[13] It is also postulated in table 27 that the administrative costs remained constant, although it is to be assumed that in fact they increased toward the close of the planning period. What did change in relation to the plan objectives and can be quantified is the total investment volume and, therefrom, the amounts of depreciation (I will continue to ignore the interest-bearing potential of these investments). The total capital outlay appears to have amounted to roughly Cub$400 million for the entire period of the plan, but little is known about allocation and financing.[14] Therefore, the total investments in our computation were allocated in equal shares to the years of the plan. The only exception is 1969, when they were tripled, since the capacity expansion in the sugar industry took place in that year.

TABLE 27. Implementation of the Financial Production Plan

Variables	1965		1966	
	Quant.	%[a]	Quant.	%[a]
Sugar cane				
Production, 10^6 t	50.7	103	36.8	70
Investments, 10^6	50	48	50	24
Sugar cane costs				
Administration, 10^6	67	100	67	100
Variable costs, 10^6	469	103	341	69
Depreciation, 10^6	—	—	2.5	25
Total costs, 10^6	536	102	411	72
Average cost/t, $	10.57	98	11.15	104
Raw sugar				
Production, 1,000 t	6,156	103	4,537	70
Industrial yield, %	12.15	98	12.32	99
Average cost/t, $	87.07	99	90.59	104
Average cost/lb., ¢	3.95	99	4.10	104

a. In percentage of plan objectives.

Taking these assumptions into account, it appears that the evolution of the average costs for sugar cane were influenced merely by differences in administrative costs and in depreciation, which explains the small deviations from the target figures. In addition, the average costs for raw sugar were determined by the industrial yield which, especially toward the end of the planning period, dropped below the target figure despite the shortfall in production. This contingency was bound to result in increased costs, irrespective of the extent to which the base cost data for sugar cane actually corresponded to reality.

In conclusion, table 28 summarizes the implementation of the hypothetical marketing plan in its financial aspects. What is to be stressed in this connection is the crumbling of sugar prices on the free international market, where the average level between 1965 and 1969 fluctuated around 2¢ per pound,[15] which covered only half the production costs. The USSR paid the contractual price throughout that period, while the other socialist countries paid between 5.31 and 6.75¢ per pound, provided one accepts the

TABLE 27 (Continued)

1967		1968		1969		1970	
Quant.	%[a]	Quant.	%[a]	Quant.	%[a]	Quant.	%[a]
50.9	83	42.8	65	41.6	55	81.0	96
50	38	50	21	150	64	50	—
67	100	67	100	67	100	67	100
471	83	397	65	385	55	750	96
5.0	24	7.5	26	10.0	26	20.0	39
543	83	472	67	462	58	837	93
10.67	100	11.02	103	11.10	104	10.33	97
6,236	83	5,165	65	4,459	50	8,538	85
12.26	100	12.19	100	11.02	91	10.71	89
87.08	100	91.35	104	103.61	116	98.03	109
3.95	100	4.14	104	4.69	116	4.44	109

computation method elaborated earlier. It is known that in 1964 China was willing to pay the same price as the Soviet Union, and events do not contradict the assumption that this remained true even after the political conflict of 1965. According to Castro in 1965, the other COMECON nations all paid a price of over 5¢ per pound.[16] The deviations in the results probably can be explained by the fact that some quantities of more expensive refined sugar were sold also, but this cannot be proven statistically.

Cuba fulfilled the sales volume target figures only on the COMECON and China market, even though the average price realized on that market lay minimally under the target figure of

TABLE 28. Implementation of the Financial Marketing Plan

	1965		1966	
Markets	Quant.	%[a]	Quant.	%[a]
Free market				
Sales volume, 10^6	80	63	48	38
Price, ¢/lb.	2.12	65	1.86	57
Closed markets				
USSR				
Sales volume, 10^6	331	117	245	60
Price, ¢/lb.	6.11	100	6.11	100
COMECON and China[b]				
Sales volume, 10^6	172	79	201	124
Average price, ¢/lb.	6.75	110	6.30	103
Subtotal				
Sales volume, 10^6	503	99	446	79
Average price, ¢/lb.	6.31	103	6.20	101
Total exports				
Revenues, 10^6	583	92	494	71
Average price, ¢/lb.	4.97	95	5.05	96
Total costs				
Exports, 10^6	463	96	402	77
Average costs, ¢/lb.	3.95	99	4.10	104
Net revenues, 10^6	120	80	92	60
Profit margin, %[c]	20.6	85	18.6	74

a. In percentage of plan objectives.
b. All socialist countries except the USSR.
c. Net revenues in percentage of export revenues.

6.11¢ per pound. The "sugar debt" of 12 million tons accumulated with the USSR between 1965 and 1970 corresponded to a loss in revenue of $1.5 billion. In contrast, on the free international market Cuba fulfilled its planned objective in terms of quantity but failed to realize the planned foreign exchange revenue from these exports because the sugar price in those years dropped to its lowest level in the postwar period. These two results are interrelated since Cuba, on the one hand, was compelled to obtain a minimum foreign currency revenue even when the sugar price was dropping on the free international market while, on the other hand,

TABLE 28 (Continued)

1967		1968		1969		1970	
Quant.	%ᵃ	Quant.	%ᵃ	Quant.	%ᵃ	Quant.	%ᵃ
77	61	62	49	115	80	174	108
1.99	61	1.98	61	2.70	83	3.75	115
333	62	247	37	182	27	419	62
6.11	100	6.11	100	6.11	100	6.11	100
177	114	170	115	188	107	199	73
5.52	90	5.64	92	5.59	91	5.31	87
510	73	417	55	370	44	618	65
5.88	96	5.90	97	5.90	97	5.83	95
587	71	479	54	485	49	792	72
4.68	87	4.71	87	4.58	85	5.19	96
495	82	421	65	497	67	677	82
3.95	100	4.14	104	4.69	116	4.44	109
92	42	58	25	− 12	− 5	115	42
15.7	58	9.6	36	−2.4	− 8	14.5	58

the shift in the quantitative export shares, exacerbated by the shortfall in production, was made entirely at the expense of the Soviet market.

The consequences are apparent in the fulfillment ratio of the target export revenue figures: Instead of a planned total of $5.1 billion, Cuba only realized $3.4 billion, while the profit margin showed a simultaneous downward trend due to the increase in average production costs.[17]

The Zafra of 1965

In connection with the launching of the great sugar offensive, 1965 was declared the "Year of Agriculture." In the preceding year fertilizer application in cane cultivation had been increased sharply though the surface of cultivated land was expanded only insignificantly. The climatic conditions were excellent, so that favorable harvest forecasts were made as early as the beginning of the year.[18] Altogether more than 50 million tons of cane were harvested, more than had been foreseen in the plan's objectives, although the surface of the crop land was somewhat smaller than planned. As a consequence, the agricultural yield was also above the target figure of 45 tons per hectare.

The harvested crop proved sufficient for a production of 6.150 million tons of raw sugar, so that the production projection was exceeded from the very start of the planning period. The only drawback was that the extraction rate of 12.12 percent was not fully satisfactory and entailed an increase in the average production costs for raw sugar.

The harvest lasted 130 working days, somewhat less than expected. Just under 400,000 tons of cane were processed daily, corresponding to fairly high utilization of the installed capacity without any bottlenecks. The utilization rate of 71 percent was never to be realized again.

For the first time the harvesting process was partly mechanized on a large scale. Even though a fraction of the *zafra* was brought in by harvesting combines on an experimental basis, this was of little consequence for the results achieved. On the other hand, one-fourth of the total cane cut was already being loaded in the field by mechanical means, and the first *centros de acopio* were tested. Nevertheless, the savings in manpower obviously were only minimal, and volunteers for the harvest had to be mobilized on a large scale. For the first time, army units also were assigned to participate in the *zafra*. If one assumes that the productivity corresponded to the estimate indicated in the computation, the seasonal workers numbered roughly 250,000, one-third of whom were volunteers who had been promised financial bonuses in case of high performance.[19]

The exceptionally favorable harvest result could not be turned into a corresponding gain in the foreign trade balance, however. The Soviet Union bought roughly 2.5 million tons of sugar, more than had been foreseen in the plan, while the remaining socialist countries bought somewhat less than had been expected. All in all, the socialist countries bought $0.5 billion worth of sugar, more or less in line with the Cuban projections. On the basis of given computations, the average price equaled 6.30¢ per pound, more than the target figure. Apart from probable exports of some refined sugar, this deviation may also be explained by the possibility that Cuba may have succeeded in selling on the free international market at a price slightly higher than the average level. If this was indeed the case, the assumed price for the socialist countries must be revised downward.

Meanwhile, the sugar price on the free international market had disintegrated dramatically, dropping at times to a low of 1.60¢ per pound, until it found its level at 2.12¢. The FAO ascribed this evolution to the sharp rise in the offer of sugar in the wake of the price increases during the preceding years. Indeed, world sugar production in 1964–65 had increased by one-fifth in comparison with the preceding year, and by one-third in relation to the 1962–63 figures.[20]

Nevertheless, Cuba sold 1.7 million tons of sugar on the free international market, more than had been foreseen, and precisely because of the drop in price. Thus, the foreign exchange derived from these sales, amounting to a mere $80 million, in truth corresponded to only 60 percent of the target figure and lowered the total sugar export revenue to roughly $580 million. This was even less than in the preceding year, despite the increased production figures. The profit margin, together with the profitability of the sugar exports as viewed in the framework of overall economic management, at the same time sank to 20 percent, making it clear that Cuba was not immune to the effects of unfavorable evolutions of the sugar price on the free international market. This experience subsequently was to repeat itself much more pronouncedly. For even then it became unavoidable to increase the share in exports to the free international market at the expense of exports to the socialist bloc—though not as yet of those to the USSR—which was bound to reduce overall export revenues.

Apparently Cuba anticipated quite early a possible crumbling of the sugar price on the free international market and took great pains not to accelerate the process by increasing its offer of sugar. Therefore, Castro announced in 1965 that the expansion of sugar production was to serve almost exclusively exports to the socialist countries.[21] In the long run, however, he expected that Cuba's competitors on the free international market eventually would eliminate themselves by cutting each other's throats.

This assumption proved a miscalculation. No other country in the world was geared as exclusively to sugar production as Cuba and, consequently, absorbed so small a share of its total sugar output on the domestic market; yet it is precisely through the domestic market and by means of appropriate protective tariff measures that, at least theoretically and partially, a shortage of revenues from the foreign market could be compensated. Moreover, no other country was as dependent as Cuba, both in absolute terms and in relation to its total sales, on exports to the free sugar market. On the contrary, the exclusion of Cuba from the U.S. sugar market brought about a situation in which countries such as the Dominican Republic, which had been excessively dependent on the free market, benefited from the redistribution of the former Cuban sugar quota and were able to shift their sugar exports from the free market to that of the United States.

Thus, the free international market, after the elimination of Cuba from the U.S. sugar market, had also become a residual market for all the other cane-producing countries and, as a result, the sugar price "bears not the faintest relationship to costs of production, or to decent living standards. It is simply a dumping price and is so recognized universally."[22]

The Zafra of 1966

During the preceding year it had become obvious that the production objective of 6 million tons could not be fulfilled.[23] Exceptionally dry weather during the maturation of the sugar cane made it probable that neither the agricultural nor the industrial yield would meet expectations. The infrequency of situation reports by the Cuban leadership to their people may be considered an indication of the poor progress of the harvest. The preceding year, frequent progress reports had been given, and Castro had announced that the cane area would be enlarged by 30 percent and had made public for the first time the production objectives up to 1970.[24]

On the basis of the target agricultural yield, the harvesting of a total quantity set at 53 million tons of sugar cane would have required an expansion of the harvest area to 1.130 million hectares. However, only 200,000 hectares were newly planted in 1965, without specifying how much of that area had not been cane land previously. The conversion of six-year-old stubble cane alone would have required 160,000 hectares of the cane land previously cultivated, so that only 40,000 hectares remained for additional planting. It is highly probable, therefore, that the total available harvest area already was too small for fulfillment of production objectives.

In fact, only 979,000 hectares ultimately were harvested that year, less than at any time after the revolution, and only 68 percent of the objective. Despite the continued increase in fertilizer application, the agricultural yield dropped by 10 tons as compared with the preceding year. The total harvest only amounted to 37 million tons of sugar cane and thus corresponded to the 1964 level. What reasons may have contributed to this setback beyond the unfavorable climatic conditions—which, however, cannot be compared with the devastating effects of Hurricane Flora in that earlier year—can only be surmised.

Nevertheless, a satisfactory industrial yield of 12.32 percent made it possible to achieve a production volume which, with 4.5 million tons of sugar, was somewhat higher than in 1964. The harvest only lasted 102 working days and, in view of the lower daily performance, probably required less manpower than in the preceding year, or around 240,000 workers, on the basis of previous computations. Meanwhile the number of *macheteros*, the professional cane cutters, already had dropped to 147,000, which no longer was sufficient to bring in the average daily harvest.[25] Therefore, volunteers and army units again had to be commandeered in 1966 for the harvest, despite its small size.

The mechanization of the harvesting operation remained within the modest scope of the preceding year. Only in the loading phase had labor substitution made some progress through the introduction of dredge-type loading cranes: 44 percent of the total cane volume was lifted by mechanical means, which probably compensated to some degree the unavoidable drop in productivity caused by the increased use of volunteers.[26] A two-year test had shown that Soviet combines could not solve the problem of mechanization. They were economically unsuitable, particularly because impurities reached the processing plants with the cut cane and placed a great strain on the installations. In addition, they required expensive preparation of the harvesting area. Instead, the *centros de acopio* increasingly proved to be the most suitable compromise solution for Cuban conditions, since they were able to improve the industrial yield by cleaning the dry cane already in the field. On the strength of these experiences, Fidel Castro proclaimed for the future the massive introduction of such harvesting stations.[27] At the same time he emphasized that the true meaning of mechanization was to be found not so much in the rationalization but in the "humanization" of labor, which would allow a reduction, not necessarily in the number of workers, but in the numbers of hours worked.

Indeed, the precondition for any increase in daily harvest performance would have been an increase in industrial processing capacity. However, any such improvement effort remained dependent largely on the import potential from capitalist countries, a potential which, for the time being, was severely curtailed by the low price of sugar.

Cuba exported a total of slightly over 4.4 million tons of sugar in 1966. Taking into account domestic requirements, this could only have been possible through a sharp reduction in existing inventories. Some 3.2 million tons were sold in the socialist markets, but once again only 60 percent of the Soviet quota was actually used. The export revenue from the socialist markets amounted to $440 million. If Cuba, as projected, had been able to sell 4.2 million tons (or almost all its sugar exports) to the socialist countries, the total revenue would have been higher by at least $90 million. Actually, this revenue only amounted to barely $0.5 billion, since the sugar price on the free market had dropped to 1.86¢ per pound. Even though Cuba curtailed exports to the Western nations by half a million tons in relation to the preceding year, it could not dispense with a minimum foreign currency revenue which by now had sunk to only 38 percent of the projected figure. This fact, together with the Soviet Union's readiness to grant credit, explains why Cuba was unable to sell at optimum revenue conditions at the very time when its export production was decreasing. Instead, it became obvious that the proportionate share of sales on the free sugar market tended to rise as sugar production decreased.

A glance at the profitability calculation shows that when assuming constant variable marginal costs, the fixed-cost share had increased and was reflected in turn in an increase of the unit cost for raw sugar to 4¢ per pound. Since the sugar price on the free international market was less than half that amount, the profitability of sugar production had to be ensured exclusively by exports to the socialist markets, where the profit margin still amounted to 18.6 percent. Therefore, any shift of exports at the expense of the socialist markets, caused by continued stagnation of production and the perennial shortage of foreign currency, was bound to thrust the Cuban sugar economy to the very edge of economic viability. If Cuba had sold sugar in 1966 on the free international market to the same extent as in the preceding year —as had been announced[28]—then the total revenues would have been decreased by an additional $40 million. At that point, and in view of the presumably excessively low estimate of production costs, the Cuban sugar economy would have been perilously close to the break-even point.

The highly unsatisfactory overall results of the 1966 *zafra,* in my opinion, were of decisive importance for the entire further evolution of the implementation of the sugar plan. Cuba could do little about the price evolution on the world market, which must be ascribed to an international policy somewhat analogous to the so-called pork cycle. However, in contrast to the preceding year, production results had fallen far short of the objectives, not only because of climatic conditions but also because of failure to take a series of preparatory measures, particularly the planting of new sugar cane. If the target figures of the plan still were to be fulfilled by 1970, efforts toward an intensification and expansion of cane cultivation had to be undertaken right away. Likewise, investment programs had to be initiated without delay for the expansion of the processing industry. Insofar as this involved capital goods from the Soviet Union, it did not entail any problems in procurement. This is shown by the fact that harvest mechanization could be attempted to the extent elaborated in the preceding pages. On the other hand, the potential for investment goods required for the expansion of industry was severely curtailed by meager export sales in the West.

The Zafra of 1967

The sugar plan for 1967 anticipated exceeding the absolute record set by the 1952 harvest, in which roughly 60 million tons of cane, harvested in 136 working days, had been processed into 7.3 million tons of raw sugar, corresponding to a daily performance of 442,000 tons.[29] These results could not be achieved. Instead, the 1967 zafra equaled that of 1965 in terms of quantity production indicators. To harvest 60 million tons of sugar cane, 1.250 million hectares of cane land would have been required. Data from the preceding year relating to the extent of new areas under cultivation once more indicate that not enough crop land was available. A mere 170,000 hectares were plowed up and planted in 1966, of which a major portion must have been used simply to replace stubble cane. Otherwise the failure of such a conversion to cana planta would have led to a drop in the agricultural yield. Despite complaints about allegedly adverse climatic conditions, the agricultural yield was the only result that corresponded to the target figures and, at 49 tons, should be considered very high for Cuban standards.

The overall harvested area was slightly smaller than in 1965, but the yield in terms of weight was somewhat higher. The harvest period of 133 days was also minimally longer. On the other hand, daily performance was smaller, so that the utilization of installed capacity was lower.[30] The number of harvest workers again amounted to 250,000, assuming that the continued decline in the number of professional cane cutters could be neutralized more or less by wider mechanization of the harvesting operation.

By then, 7 percent of all cane was being processed by the *centros de acopio,* and more than 50 percent was loaded mechanically; but 98 percent still was being cut manually, since the harvesting combines continued to operate unsatisfactorily.

The industrial yield of 12.26 percent was close to the target figure. Thus, despite the fact that the production of 6.2 million tons of raw sugar only corresponded to 83 percent of the objective, Castro's only comment on April 19—"Marcha bien la Zafra"—expressed satisfaction but no outright enthusiasm.[31]

The financial revenue of $587 million realized from sugar production also equaled that of 1965. Despite the still depressed level of sugar prices, 1.7 million tons were again traded on the free international market, though this brought in an even lower revenue in foreign exchange than two years earlier. A further 2.5 million tons were bought by the Soviet Union, so that once again less than two-thirds of the Soviet export quota was actually utilized, despite the—by then—even greater price differential in relation to the other types of market. The remaining socialist countries bought the same volume as in the preceding year, but the contractual clearing price now only amounted to 5.52¢ per pound, a figure which is to be accepted with the usual reservations.

Thus it became clear that the reduction in exports to the free sugar market noted for the preceding year was to remain the exception. If the sugar plan was not to be abandoned altogether, the planned investment measures had to be implemented in earnest. Therefore, an emergency plan was elaborated so as to catch up with all that had been neglected up to that point.[32] Even though the 1967 *zafra* could not be increased decisively, it had become imperative to obtain larger amounts of foreign currency to implement measures for which imports from the West—not least among these, fertilizers—were essential. Thus, even in 1967, the increase in the volume of exports was distributed evenly between the socialist countries and the free international market.

With respect to the profitability of these exports, this shift resulted in a total export revenue which exceeded the costs by a bare 16 percent, thus further reducing the profit margin in comparison with that of the preceding year. Therefore, the difference from the *zafra* of 1965 was to be found mainly in the profitability calculation, which showed that since the inception of the sugar plan the hypothetically computed net revenues had decreased continuously.

The Zafras *of 1968 and 1969*

After 1967, all efforts were concentrated primarily on ensuring the 10 million-ton harvest in 1970. This meant that attention was focused on preliminary undertakings, such as the preparation of large cultivation areas, large irrigation projects, the readying of fertilizer facilities, and so on, while current sugar production, as a result, was neglected. Every effort was made to ensure a rise in the supply of the primary product, so measures were taken principally to expand the cultivation areas and increase agricultural yield. Special attention was also directed to the agricultural factors liable to contribute to stabilizing the industrial yield, such as the selection of new cane varieties and the timing of the planting, so that optimum results might be expected in 1970.[33]

Nevertheless, the production target for the *zafra* of 1968 called for results exceeding those of the record harvest of 1952. As in the preceding year, the cultivated areas once again proved too small. The production totaled roughly 5 million tons of sugar, a volume that well may be realizable on the average but assuredly is not an optimum cost performance. What is to be noted in view of the 1970 *zafra* is that the harvest only lasted 113 days, which corresponds to processing 380,000 tons per day. This volume could be accomplished readily with the old installed capacity of 550,000 tons without encountering any bottlenecks. The harvest had not been mechanized further since 1967, so that approximately the same number of workers was required, though for a somewhat shorter time.

In terms of foreign trade figures, the decline in production performance led to grievous consequences which were to become even more pronounced in 1969, and gave rise to the question of whether one could justify sacrificing virtually the entire production of both these years to the *zafra* of 1970.

Roughly 3 million tons of sugar were traded on the socialist market, where the clearing prices agreed upon with the other countries were slightly lower than those paid by the Soviet Union. The latter only purchased 37 percent of its contractual quota, while purchases by the other members of the socialist market remained on the scale of the preceding year. But each ton of sugar sold outside the USSR on the free international market entailed a loss in revenue of $90, since the sugar price there was still below 2¢ per pound. Nevertheless, and under heavy pressure to secure foreign currency funds, Cuba sold 30 percent of its total exports on the free international market. The total revenue amounted to barely $480 million, the lowest figure realized since 1963, while the median price, despite the sales on the socialist preferential markets, sank to 4.58¢ per pound. Meanwhile, however, production costs, mainly as a consequence of the relatively low industrial yield, had climbed to 4.14¢ per pound and thus allowed for a profit margin of only 10 percent. In view of the fact that some 20 percent of the export volume consisted of refined sugar—even though refining costs have not been considered here—the Cuban sugar economy in 1968 may already have been producing below the break-even point.

On the positive side, a total of 420,000 hectares of agricultural land were newly planted with sugar cane in 1968, and this constituted an important step toward realizing the objectives of the 1970 *zafra*. Measures also were taken in earnest toward adaptation of the industrial processing capacity. Unfortunately both these undertakings were at the expense of the *zafra* of 1969, which Fidel Castro termed with some justification the "country's agony."[34]

Moreover, bottlenecks arose which were to reappear the following year.

The sugar cane harvest totaled just over 40 million tons. This modest result can be attributed in large measure to the fact that the cane newly planted in 1967 was reused in its entirety (in 1968) for planting the 1970 *zafra,* so that only stubble cane (with a lower extraction rate) was available for the 1969 harvest. Then the rainy season started early and further reduced the intensity of the harvesting operation. In 135 days the daily performance only amounted to 300,000 tons, less than in the entire annals of modern Cuban sugar production.

However, this was due not only to the circumstances just described, but also to insufficient industrial capacity. The fact is that in some plants installation work was still in progress during the harvest, so that several mills could not participate at all. In other plants, the new installations, which always require a certain starting-up time, did not operate satisfactorily, resulting in a lower industrial yield than expected.[35] Nor were shortcomings such as lack of technical competence and poor organization conducive to favorable results now that the production process had become more complex. Bottlenecks in transportation resulted from necessary changes in shipping cane to plants that originally had different supply regions, and this in turn led to undesirable delays and to longer supply routes than had been foreseen.

All these circumstances occasioned not only lower cane production but also a relatively poor processing record. The industrial yield sank to 11 percent, and the resulting loss in revenue alone, expressed in sugar volume, amounted to half a million tons compared with the preceding year—which had not been particularly good either. As a result, and in view of the high proportion of fixed costs at a low production level, it may be assumed that the average sugar costs rose to 4.7¢ per pound.

Ultimately, production amounted to a total of 4.5 million tons of raw sugar. To achieve an acceptable export revenue, existing stocks had to be further reduced, making possible the export of 4.8 million tons, a bare 60 percent of the original target figure of the plan. Of these, 1.9 million tons went to the free international market which, since 1968, was once again regulated by a sugar agreement under which the minimum contractual price of 3.25¢ per pound could be maintained on the average. In computing the Cuban foreign exchange revenue, it should be assumed, however, that the sugar actually was sold rather at 2.70¢ per pound, the lowest price for that year. Indeed, as Fidel Castro explained, Cuba was forced to sell significant quantities of sugar on the free international market even when prices were dropping because of its pressing need for capital goods, a fact that explains the extensive use made of the Cuban export quota on that market.[36]

If one were to assume instead that Cuba got the average world market price, the sugar price paid by the socialist countries, computed on the basis of the residual revenue after deduction of exports to the USSR, would appear to have dropped to 4¢ per pound. However, this seems highly unrealistic and implausible. If, on the contrary, one accepts our first hypothesis, the price level in trading with the socialist countries remained close to that of the preceding year.

While Cuban revenues from the export of raw sugar thus equaled those of the preceding year, the export costs in all probability were $75 million higher. In view of the sharp increase in average costs and the somewhat improved price level on the free international market, this loss[37] was to be ascribed unequivocally to "subjective mistakes"—to use the term employed by Castro. Neither the weather nor the impending *zafra* of the following year could explain these results adequately. Indeed, Castro promised a stringent analysis of the causes of the mistakes made so as to avoid their repetition in the future.[38] In addition to reorganization and improvements in the maintenance of industrial and transportation equipment, the expansion of the processing plants was to be given first priority. However, the remaining time available was very short. The *zafra* of 1969 cast a shadow which boded no good for the coming year.

The Ten-Million-Ton Zafra

The year 1969 had already been proclaimed the "Year of the Decisive Thrust." And, indeed, much had been done to force the attainment of this production goal, whose importance was mainly psychological. More than 1.5 million hectares of cultivated land were ready for the harvest, of which 40 percent had been prepared with *cana planta;* and additional reserves were available. Fertilizer application in 1969 had reached the record figure of 800 kilograms per hectare, which was to ensure a high agricultural yield.[39] $170 million had been spent on expansion of the processing capacity, although no data are available regarding the capacity increases in tons. Since this sum amounted to approximately half of the original investment estimates, it may be assumed that the overall technical capacity had been increased in the same quantitative proportion or possibly slightly more through the reutilization of old equipment—in my own opinion, to 620,000 tons per day.

The renovation and expansion activity concentrated mainly on plants in the eastern part of the island. A few giant plants with an installed daily capacity of 10,000 tons were under construction. These were to be the largest in the world and were to have sufficiently large supply areas to allow for their continuous operation during the entire harvest period.

A campaign was launched at the beginning of the harvest to instill in all the harvest workers the determination to ensure a high industrial yield: "All those factors were stressed which could promote a high extraction rate . . . starting with the cutting schedule, the freshness of the cane. . . . This meant that we sought to overcome all shortcomings which could have a negative effect on the sugar yield, while devoting less attention to the problems connected with the good working order of the sugar plants since these problems never had arisen before."[40]

The production schedule foresaw a slow starting-up phase beginning as early as July 14, 1969. By Christmas, the first million tons of raw sugar were to have been produced, after which an accelerated rhythm was planned to allow for the production of an additional million tons each sixteen to eighteen working days until July 15, 1970, the deadline set for the realization of the plan.

The Cuban population was being informed of the progress of the *zafra* in detail. As early as the beginning of February it was made known that difficulties with the new plants had arisen in the eastern part of the country, the crucial production area. Some of the expansion work still had not been finished, thus blocking production, while other installations were poorly adjusted and produced only low yields.[41] These shortcomings only involved the modern plants in the eastern regions of the island, which nevertheless represented 20 percent of the total capacity and, most important, drew on the largest intake area of sugar cane.

This bottleneck at the very beginning of the harvest called for a series of improvised measures and upset the entire production schedule, which had been planned with no margin for breakdowns. The daily production and harvest quotas had to be revised downward, which led to changes in the harvesting cycle, in turn entailing reductions in the industrial yield. Cane had to be rerouted to plants in less favorable locations, which resulted in regional shifts of all production schedules, placing an excessive burden on the entire transportation system. Therefore, starting in December 1969, 5,000 kilometers of new roads were built in three months for greater transport flexibility,[42] and new railroad tracks were laid as well. All this was being done when the harvest should already have reached its highest intensity.

The expansion of the plants and of the transportation system reached its peak in February, but it nevertheless proved impossible either to raise the capacity to the target level or to achieve the required processing efficiency. As a result, the 1970 *zafra* actually was produced with a smaller milling capacity than that available for the record harvest of 1952, whose historical data had been the basis of the plan for 1970.[43] This meant that the average daily harvesting performance had to be reduced, since as many as 50,000 workers at times were made idle through production back-ups. At the same time, the harvest period had to be extended further to reach the objectives of the plan.

The first million tons of raw sugar were produced on schedule by December 23, though the industrial yield up to that point only amounted to 8 percent, so the average costs must have been substantial.[44] The next million also met the scheduled quotas, but production fell slightly behind in February. However, the industrial yield of 9 percent at that point made it clear that the consumption rate of sugar cane was much higher than expected, since cane was supposed to bring an average yield of at least 12.5 percent during the peak season between January and April. Although the yield problem improved somewhat in March, after the completion of plant repair work, 60 percent of all available cane already had been cut at the end of that month, while only half of the potential ultimate production of 10.4 million tons of raw sugar had been brought in. An additional 450,000 tons of cane were still cut daily in April, but this was less than anticipated simply because the capacity of the plants could not be expanded to the proposed extent. In May the intensity of the harvesting operation fell off, since the cane supply in the large supply areas already had been exhausted, and at the same time the low (though at least stabilized) extraction rate began to drop again as a result of the reduced quality of the cane in the late harvest season.

On May 19, Castro announced that the 10 million tons could not be reached.[45] From that moment on, any insistence on the goal set previously was bound to be to the detriment of the 1971 *zafra*. While some fresh cane reserves were still available, the rainy season starting in June made the harvesting difficult and lower yields unavoidable. By July, the industrial yield had dropped to 8.62 percent, and this signaled the end of the harvest.

A total of more than 80 million tons of cane were harvested, enough to approximate the target figure if the extraction rate averaged 12 percent, a figure which had never been lower even with large harvests during the prerevolutionary period. The yield per hectare of 56 tons corresponded to the target objective, so that fulfillment of the plan would have been possible on the basis of the agricultural conditions.

The median industrial yield of only 10.7 percent makes obvious where the battle had been lost. That ultimately 8.5 million tons of raw sugar could be produced nevertheless is a surprising fact, and one that did not remain uncontested. The daily quantity of processed sugar cane amounted only to 370,000 tons—more or less the average achieved in the years preceding the plan. If we advance the rather daring assumption that labor productivity remained at the projected level, then 300,000 field workers participated continuously in the *zafra* between January and April, with an additional 100,000 workers in the plants.[46] If one averages the number of workers over the entire period of the harvest, the total figure probably should be reduced by 50,000.

If we consider the 1970 *zafra* in terms of costs and restrict this consideration for the time being to a strictly operational analysis, it appears that the production costs were approximately 10 percent above our assumed target level. Subject to the usual reservations, these costs thus amounted to 4.44¢ per pound.

Castro attempted to explain the underlying reasons for the unsatisfactory harvest results as follows:

Three factors chiefly were responsible for the low yield:
1. the new installations;
2. insufficient maintenance;
3. —and to tell the truth it is a moot question whether this is to be considered truly the third or the foremost factor—inefficient management of the plants.

Obviously our mills today are 18 years older than in 1952 . . . but we believe that age by itself is not a basic factor, . . . and that instead there is something that has deteriorated more than the plants themselves, namely the management, the operation, and the direction of the plants, resulting from the fact that many of the old workers have retired . . . and that we failed to set up an appropriate program for the replacement and training of the work force.[47]

What gives one pause, however, is the fact that these very same problems, arising from more exacting technology, already had contributed to the poor results of the 1969 *zafra* and had been identified at that time. Therefore, it was to be expected that the new installations would cause problems of adaptation in 1970, but the time then remaining apparently was too short to take preventive measures. This was the penalty for having neglected, in past years and in view of the stagnation in the growing of sugar cane, to become familiar with the problems of expanding industrial capacity. These led to bottlenecks such as those encountered in a different form in the agricultural sector whose solution had required a full four years.

Cuba exported a total of some 7 million tons of sugar in 1970. Actually, the total export volume of the 1970 *zafra* may have been slightly larger, since some backlogs in 1969 supply commitments still had to be filled. For the first time since 1962, the Soviet Union again bought over 3 million tons, though this once more corresponded to only 60 percent of its allocation. The rest of the socialist countries bought sugar in quantities close to the calculated quotas (1.7 million tons) and compensated these purchases at an estimated price of 5.31¢ per pound. On the free international market, where the price was now rising slowly (3.75¢ per pound), Cuba sold more than 2 million tons. More than half was allocated to Japan, which thereby realized the plan for an increase in its own consumption and, thus, in its net imports.

The total revenue for the year from all types of markets totaled roughly $800 million, which corresponds to more than 70 percent of the target figure.

If we attempt in conclusion to assess the export profitability of the "Great *Zafra*" on the basis of export costs totaling $680 million, we arrive in spite of everything at a profit margin of 15 percent. While the unit price was only 9 percent above the target figure, this in my view is unduly optimistic, since the refining costs of at least 600,000 tons of exported refined sugar had not been taken into consideration. Likewise, the administrative costs (herein assumed to have remained constant) were surely underestimated similarly.

In spite of everything, the *zafra* of 1970 realized its chief original objective, an increase in import capability, to a greater extent than the harvests of the preceding years. That the external costs were bound to be high as a result of the total economic effort will be elaborated in greater detail in the final section.

Concluding Comments on the Sugar Plan

Before analyzing the macroeconomic consequences of the sugar plan and its implementation, I will attempt an overall critical assessment of the plan as a whole.

In the first place, the plan was overly optimistic in the determination of its objectives, a judgment which requires no special corroboration. If, moreover—as I believe—the plan truly was meant to be in the nature of general instructions, it proved to be a highly inflexible policy-shaping instrument. It would have been more appropriate as a guideline for possible modifications of yearly objectives in the light of experience, which alone can determine ex post facto the difference between what is desirable and what is possible. Such a concept would have amounted to what is commonly called a sliding plan.

In fact, the yearly production targets hardly were made dependent on the results of preceding planning periods. To cite but one example, despite the fact that the expansion of industrial processing capacity and future production potential were linked to past foreign exchange revenues, the original and overly ambitious target figures were maintained even when the sugar price on the world market fluctuated for long periods around 2¢ per pound. In the agricultural sector it is equally evident that the planned annual objectives for the production of sugar cane depended on the cane area prepared for cultivation in the preceding year. Yet each year of the plan brought the monotonous revelation that the planted area of the preceding year was inadequate for the established production targets. Thus, the plan was inflexible in that it failed to consider cogent and constant time contingencies.

Moreover, the criterion of internal consistency seems to have been neglected. Thus, it became particularly obvious in 1969 and 1970 that the industrial capacity had been adapted insufficiently to the needs of the prepared agricultural production because—in Castro's own words—"this had never been a problem before."

Up to 1968, these shortcomings were of no great relevance simply because, judging from the results, the sugar plan never had been followed with any stringency. If one were to impute to this preliminary phase the realizations formulated in a policy-shaping plan, it would have to bear the title "Plan for the Consolidation of Prerevolutionary Production Levels."

The sugar plan became truly significant only in 1969. From a purely economic viewpoint, there were indeed cogent reasons (in particular, the growing deficit in the balance of payments) which made a drastic increase in export production seem highly desirable. However, political factors may have been even more imperative in that the achievements of the revolution were to be documented not only in its social but also in its economic consequences. Thus, Castro stated as late as 1970:

If we fail to achieve the 10 million [tons] . . . we shall suffer a moral defeat. . . . This time it is a whole nation who is to make a superhuman effort to reach a goal which shall be raised as the banner for what we stand for, the banner of socialism, and for which we have fought with a determination with which all revolutionaries need fight to achieve their goals.[48]

This political commitment, invoked many times in the same breath with the call for victory over imperialism by the Vietnamese and Cambodian people, now meant that the 10 million tons of production had to be forced through without any consideration for economic costs.

If instead they had tried to raise production gradually and without undue haste until 1970 with the available means, then there is no reason to doubt that the *zafra* of 1969 (with a normal share of *cana planta* and the previously installed capacity) could have brought the same result as the preceding year with a similarly shortened harvest of comparable intensity. Nor can it be doubted that 7 million tons could have been produced in 1970 with proper maintenance of existing installations. In the end, the total volume of the two harvests, 13 million tons, would have been the same as the one actually realized; but it would have been achieved with a saving of $200 million because of the higher industrial yield made possible.[49] More important still, the external costs to the national economy in 1970 could have been avoided. As Castro had warned prophetically: "If we should fail to work simultaneously and with the same degree of efficiency on all agricultural fronts, the struggle for the 10 million tons is bound to end in a Pyrrhic victory."[50]

If we assess the achievement of the sugar economy in the light of the given marketing structure and under the criterion of profitability over the entire period of the plan, it becomes evident that, despite all negative factors, Cuba between 1965 and 1970 produced significantly above the (theoretical) break-even point.[51]

Foreign Trade

The Development of the Commodity Structure

The immediate goal of the sugar plan had been an increase in import capability. Concentration on the sugar economy had been grounded on comparative cost advantages, but similar advantages could also be claimed for other products. Therefore, the aim was to achieve a diversification of exports simultaneously with the expansion of the sugar economy.

A glance at a compilation of all exports reveals that this endeavor was only marginally successful (table 29). Exports of citrus fruit, as well as of canned fruit and vegetables, could be raised somewhat, as is also true for exports of tobacco, beverages, and, particularly, fish. Nevertheless, sugar and its by-products accounted on the average for 95 percent of all basic and nonessential food exports.[52] On the whole, however, the share of this class of commodities dropped in 1970 to 80 percent of the total export volume. This slight shift favored the export of raw materials as a result of the sharp increase in the mining of nickel. These nickel deposits already had been exploited in the prerevolutionary period and, originally, had been considered as a possible alternative investment object to sugar production;[53] but finally, and in view of the lengthy development period involved, only limited investments were made in this sector. This cautious approach now bore early fruit in that the exports of nickel increased from $42 million (1964) to $172 million (1970).[54]

Otherwise Cuba had few commodities to offer on the international market. In the last analysis, sugar was to keep its preponderant share in the export field; between 1964 and 1969, which are to be regarded as average years, it accounted for a median share of 82.5 percent. This meant that throughout the period of the present analysis the monetary value of the total export volume was subject to strong fluctuations resulting from the sharply varying performances of the sugar economy. Parallel with sales results on the world sugar market, the revenues from total exports between 1964 and 1969 showed a tendency toward stagnation. It was only in 1970 that an increase of 40 percent over the preceding year could be achieved.

In contrast, the monetary value of imports rose steadily after 1965 (see table 30). The emphasis on the cultivation of sugar cane and on cattle-breeding had made it necessary to forgo the growing of other crops for the domestic market. Therefore, imports of food products had to continue. Their monetary value up to 1969 amounted to roughly $200 million but jumped abruptly to $250

TABLE 29. Commodity Structure in Foreign Trade, Exports (million $ f.o.b.)

	1963		1964		1965	
	Amt.	%	Amt.	%	Amt.	%
Food products	479	88	631	89	597	87
Beverages and tobacco	22	4	30	4	33	5
Raw materials	34	7	42	6	51	7
Prod. goods	2	0	2	0	0	0
Miscellaneous	7	1	9	1	10	1
Total	544	100	714	100	691	100

Sources: JUCEPLAN, Boletín Estadístico 1968 (Havana, n.d.), pp. 150 ff.; JUCEPLAN, Boletín Estadístico 1970 (Havana, n.d.), pp. 192–93.

million in 1970. The chief products in this class of commodities were grain and dairy products, which could not be reduced in quantity despite the priority granted to the promotion of the cattle industry.[55]

As in the case of exports, the overall composition of imports remained relatively stable: Food products required approximately 20 percent of the import capability; fuel an almost constant 9 percent; machines and means of transportation (up to 1969) between 14 and 17 percent. Nor did the shares of all other imported commodities show any appreciable changes. This means that no statistically significant import substitutions had been achieved in any of the listed commodity categories. On the contrary, a tendency toward increase could be observed in the chief import commodities, and what varied was merely their rate of increase. One gains the overall impression that the commodity structure of the imports had shifted slightly in favor of capital goods, but this increase was not offset by an absolute reduction in the import of consumer goods.

As a result of the relatively inelastic demand, the evolution of imports registered a smaller fluctuation range than the exports but followed a relatively uniform slope, even though the increase between 1963 and 1970 ($1.3 billion) amounted to a total of 50 percent. But since the export revenues during that same period,

TABLE 29 (Continued)

1966		1967		1968		1969		1970	
Amt.	%	Amt.	%	Amt.	%	Amt.	%	Amt.	%
511	85	608	87	507	79	516	79	825	79
28	5	31	4	40	6	45	7	35	3
46	8	54	8	80	12	92	13	172	17
2	0	1	0	2	0	2	0	1	0
11	2	8	1	22	3	9	1	10	1
598	100	702	100	651	100	664	100	1,043	100

with the exception of the last statistically covered year, had remained stagnant, the trade balance deficit also rose steadily. The accumulated debt toward foreign countries amounted to $2.5 billion, which corresponds approximately to the revenues realized for all sugar exports between 1966 and 1970.

The primary macroeconomic consequences of the sugar plan can be summarized as follows: Up to 1969, the export volume had hardly increased at all. The one-sided promotion of the sugar economy was incompatible with any significant diversification of exports. The concentration on the sugar economy spurred the demand for imports, and efforts toward substitution could not keep pace with this evolution. The result was a growing deficit in the trade balance.

In conclusion, in terms of foreign exchange, the sugar plan amounted to a jump out of the frying pan into the fire. However, these poor results were due in major part to unfavorable conditions on the sugar market. The territorial structure of foreign trade and the corresponding terms of trade will clarify to what extent Cuba itself had to bear the external costs entailed by the sugar plan.

TABLE 30. Commodity Structure in Foreign Trade, Imports (million $ c.i.f.)

	1963		1964		1965	
	Amt.	%	Amt.	%	Amt.	%
Food products	192	22	224	22	182	21
Beverages and tobacco	0	0	1	0	1	0
Raw materials	25	3	36	4	25	3
Fuel	77	9	87	9	85	10
Animal and vegetable fats	16	2	19	2	22	3
Chemicals	52	6	66	6	39	4
Prod. goods	128	15	152	15	148	17
Machines and means of transportation	119	14	138	14	133	15
Various consumer goods	4	0	6	0	6	1
Miscellaneous	254	29	290	28	226	26
Total	867	100	1,019	100	867	100

Sources: JUCEPLAN, *Boletín Estadístico 1968* (Havana, n.d.), pp. 153 ff.; JUCEPLAN, *Boletín Estadístico* 1970 (Havana, n.d.), pp. 192–93.

The Evolution of the Territorial Structure

Cuba classified its foreign markets according to monetary policy considerations and, as a secondary criterion, according to pricing conditions in the trade of goods (see table 31). On the basis of these two characteristics, Cuban statistics differentiated among three types of foreign markets:[56]

1. "Freely Convertible [Currencies]." This included all countries which paid for Cuban exports in foreign currencies or who insisted on foreign currency payments in exchange for

their own exports to Cuba. World market prices essentially applied to this type of trade, a fact which, in terms of the general trend, called on the part of Cuba for an equalized trade balance on a multilateral level with these trading partners. All the nonsocialist European countries, with the exception of Spain, belonged to this type of market, as did Japan and Canada, the most important trading partners.

TABLE 30 (Continued)

1966		1967		1968		1969		1970	
Amt.	%	Amt.	%	Amt.	%	Amt.	%	Amt.	%
191	21	212	22	210	19	212	18	249	19
1	0	0	0	0	0	0	0	1	0
36	4	41	4	45	4	33	3	44	3
92	9	93	9	93	9	106	9	113	9
21	2	24	2	29	3	20	2	20	2
62	7	100	10	99	9	77	7	93	7
147	16	141	15	134	12	150	13	171	13
131	14	162	16	186	17	189	16	242	19
6	1	7	1	5	0	5	0	5	0
239	26	203	21	288	27	376	32	362	28
926	100	983	100	1,089	100	1,168	100	1,300	100

2. "Capitalist Agreements." Trading in this type of market operated on a clearing basis, again using world market prices to determine exchange rates. In distinction to the markets of type 1, the Cuban trade balance with these trading partners had to be equalized bilaterally. The most important members of this type of market were Spain, Morocco, and the United Arab Republic.

3. "Socialist Agreements." This type of market comprised all the socialist countries, including Yugoslavia. In this case, goods essentially were compensated bilaterally by other goods. World market prices were to apply as a clearing basis for Cuban imports, while a subsidized price was to be paid for

Cuban exports. In distinction to the markets of type 2, Cuba in this case could incur bilateral indebtedness.

Between 1963 and 1970, 27 percent of all Cuban exports went to countries outside the socialist bloc. In imports, the share of the markets of types 1 and 2 reached just about 25 percent. Quantitatively speaking, the significance of the nonsocialist countries for the foreign trade of Cuba therefore was relatively small. But in fact they were of the utmost importance, since Cuba bought in the West all those goods which were unavailable in the socialist countries. As far as can be deduced from a Cuban 1968 trade balance sheet (reconstructed on the basis of statistics of countries where Cuban imports originated and which were receiving Cuban exports), the Western countries exported chiefly industrial products, such as chemicals, rubber, and textile goods, as well as various raw materials. But the largest share was that of food products, with 16 percent of the total volume in monetary terms.[57]

Among the countries belonging to markets of type 1, Cuba's most important trade partner was Japan. In 1970, 10 percent of all exports were allocated to that market, whose main function for Cuba was presumably to provide a source of foreign currency. Japan remained the only country with which Cuba was able to achieve a sizable surplus in exports, ending the eight years under scrutiny with a positive balance of bilateral trade of $211 million. Great Britain, France, and the German Federal Republic consistently imported less from Cuba than they exported. Their exports consisted mainly of industrial goods; thus, typical of today's Havana streets are British Leyland buses. The currency revenue surplus from the Japanese market was more than exhausted in trade with the industrial nations of the West, so that Cuba's multilateral foreign trade deficit in the markets of type 1 amounted to $582 million.

Almost one-quarter of this deficit accumulated by Cuba over eight years resulted from the last year under scrutiny, in which Cuban foreign trade achieved a record volume. Moreover, the

TABLE 31. Territorial Structure of Foreign Trade, by Monetary Zones
(millions of Cuban pesos)

	1963	1964	1965	1966	1967	1968	1969	1970
1. Convertible currencies								
GFR								
Exports	0	1	1	1	1	2	1	1
Imports	12	19	5	6	12	11	31	31
Balance	− 12	− 18	− 4	− 5	− 11	− 9	− 30	− 30
France								
Exports	2	3	10	10	15	15	13	14
Imports	6	19	19	13	41	67	49	59
Balance	− 4	− 16	− 9	− 3	− 26	− 52	− 36	− 45
Japan								
Exports	21	50	21	15	18	23	65	106
Imports	5	41	4	5	9	3	10	31
Balance	16	9	17	10	9	20	55	75
Great Britain								
Exports	23	26	13	12	13	14	14	19
Imports	11	38	50	25	28	30	40	59
Balance	12	− 12	− 37	− 13	− 15	− 16	− 26	− 40
Other countries								
Exports	63	57	47	23	28	50	55	72
Imports	90	140	63	46	73	70	83	166
Balance	− 27	− 83	− 16	− 23	− 45	− 20	− 28	− 94
Subtotals								
Exports	109	137	92	61	75	104	148	212
Imports	124	257	141	95	163	181	213	346
Balance	− 15	−120	− 49	− 34	− 88	− 77	− 65	−134

TABLE 31 (Continued)

	1963	1964	1965	1966	1967	1968	1969	1970
2. "Capitalist Agreements"								
Subtotals								
Exports	70	156	62	55	55	58	69	62
Imports	39	70	66	91	44	34	66	51
Balance	31	86	− 4	− 36	11	24	3	11
3. "Socialist Agreements"								
USSR								
Exports	164	275	323	274	366	290	233	529
Imports	461	410	428	521	569	667	660	687
Balance	−297	−135	−105	−247	−203	−377	−427	−158
GDR								
Exports	40	16	28	31	36	36	38	49
Imports	36	38	25	36	50	39	43	50
Balance	4	− 22	3	− 5	− 14	− 3	− 5	− 1
Bulgaria								
Exports	9	15	21	19	24	25	27	29
Imports	5	12	16	28	20	30	25	23
Balance	4	3	5	− 9	4	− 5	2	6
Czechoslovakia								
Exports	38	15	46	46	41	41	43	49
Imports	55	64	36	36	35	39	29	30
Balance	− 17	− 49	10	10	6	2	14	19
Hungary								
Exports	12	0	2	2	4	4	5	4
Imports	12	15	8	7	4	3	3	5
Balance	0	− 15	− 6	− 5	0	1	2	− 1

Poland								
Exports	18	8	4	13	6	7	7	5
Imports	29	21	8	9	7	4	4	3
Balance	−11	−13	−4	4	1	3	3	2
Rumania								
Exports	7	0	1	1	1	8	10	13
Imports	7	8	4	3	1	9	25	13
Balance	0	−8	−3	−2	0	−1	−15	0
Other countries, incl. China								
Exports	79	93	112	96	94	77	84	91
Imports	99	124	134	99	90	90	99	92
Balance	−20	−31	−22	−3	4	−13	−15	−1
Subtotals								
Exports	367	422	537	482	572	488	447	769
Imports	704	692	659	739	776	873	888	903
Balance	−337	−270	−122	−257	−204	−385	−441	−134
Totals								
Exports	546	715	691	598	702	650	664	1,043
Imports	867	1,019	866	925	983	1,088	1,167	1,300
Balance	−321	−304	−175	−327	−281	−438	−503	−257

Source: JUCEPLAN, *Boletín Estadístico 1970* (Havana, n.d.), pp. 189–91.

extent to which Cuba was granted credits by the industrial nations of the West is surprising. This made it possible, even in the absence of extensive sugar markets, to by-pass at least partially the economic embargo imposed by the United States. A total of 38 percent of all Cuban imports from the countries of type 1 could not be compensated by export revenues and, therefore, had to be financed by credits.[58]

Cuba's trade with countries of type 2 mainly held political importance, cementing friendly relations with countries of the so-called Third World. To this category belonged the United Arab Republic and Algeria, while Argentina and Mexico were significant as key points in trade with Latin America. Spain, the partner with the largest share in Cuba's trading in this type of market, owed its significance, irrespective of all ideological differences, mainly to the traditional economic and social ties between the two countries. Altogether, Cuba between 1963 and 1970 exported 10 percent of its total export volume to markets of type 2 and received from these 6 percent of its imports. Thus, the multilateral trade balance showed a slight surplus in favor of Cuba.

The preponderant share of Cuba's foreign trade was carried out with the socialist countries. From 1963 to 1970, this share amounted to 73 percent of all exports and 75 percent of all imports. Since the monetary value of exports only covered 70 percent of the import costs, the Cuban foreign debt mainly fell to the socialist countries. Ultimately, the cumulative negative balance in multilateral trade with markets of type 3 amounted to over $2 billion, or roughly 35 percent of the monetary value of the imports.

A special position among Cuba's socialist trading partners was reserved for the Soviet Union. Between 30 and 51 percent of the yearly Cuban exports were shipped across the Atlantic to the Soviet Union on Soviet freighters. Cuba mainly supplied raw sugar and received in compensation crude oil, food products, and industrial finished and semifinished products, of which neither quantities nor descriptions need be given here.[59] The import monopoly held by the USSR in energy fuels alone makes obvious the dependence on that country of the Cuban national economy.

As mentioned earlier, Cuba did not adhere to its (sugar) export commitments to the Soviet Union. Nevertheless, the latter supplied goods for a total clearing amount corresponding to that established in the agreement of 1964 according to which Cuba, by 1970, was to have exported raw sugar (24.1 million tons) valued at $3.250 billion. However, only 54 percent of that quota was actually fulfilled, so that the export shortfall amounted roughly to $1.5 billion. For the same period, the cumulative negative balance of Cuban trade with the USSR amounted to $1.652 billion. This means, on the one hand, that in monetary terms Cuba's import capacity with regard to the Soviet Union remained at the projected level, and, on the other hand, that the burden of the shortage in revenues resulting from the failure to fulfill the objectives of the sugar plan could be shifted in its entirety to the USSR.

Paradoxically, the readiness of the Soviet Union to grant credit had negative consequences for Cuba's foreign trade balance. If Cuba had complied with the contractual Soviet sugar import quota without regard to the production backlogs in the sugar economy and, thus, had allocated its sugar exports exclusively to the USSR, the Cuban foreign debt would have been reduced considerably as a result of the higher price agreed to with the USSR. However, such an optimum export allocation was ruled out because the Soviet Union could not satisfy Cuban import requirements fully. Therefore, Cuba was compelled to switch these requirements to other markets on which the imports were financed by sugar exports at the expense of the Soviet market.

It turned out, however, that in economic terms Cuba's massive indebtedness to the USSR held only statistical significance. In view of the large gap in the Cuban trade balance, the two partner nations concluded an agreement in 1972 according to which the interest-free credits granted to Cuba by the USSR in the past decade were to be paid off over a period of twenty-five years, starting in 1985. This means that the Soviet assistance was actually granted without much hope of recovery.[60]

Cuban trade with the other socialist countries approximated the volume of its trade with markets of type 1, but one gains the impression that in this case the principle of equalizing the trade balance was being observed more rigorously. Thus, while Cuba up to 1964 was a debtor of Czechoslovakia, this trade continuously showed a surplus in exports in the subsequent years up to 1970. The same held true for trade with Poland, Hungary, and Rumania which, however, never assumed any statistical significance. Among the COMECON member nations, apart from the Soviet Union and Czechoslovakia, the German Democratic Republic was the most important trading partner, with a trade volume more or less equal to that of Spain.

Unfortunately, little is known of Cuba's trade with China. The one known fact is that, within the socialist bloc and next to the USSR, China constituted Cuba's most important sugar market. If we assume that Cuba achieved balanced trade conditions with all those nations listed in table 31 as "Other Socialist Countries" (Yugoslavia, Albania, North Korea, North Vietnam, and Mongolia), then we may conjecture that China granted Cuba credit assistance in the amount of $100 million,[61] which would imply that, despite all differences in political ideology, China made a substantial contribution to the Cuban economy.

The Terms of Trade

The basis for the analysis of the territorial structure of Cuban foreign trade had been the assumption that world market prices applied to the imports from all types of markets. There is no reason to doubt that this was the case for markets of types 1 and 2. As regards markets of type 3, particularly Cuban trade with the USSR, an apposite confirmation can be found in article 7 of the trade agreement between Cuba and the USSR of February 17, 1965: "It is agreed that the prices for goods supplied reciprocally are to be established by the Soviet and Cuban importers on the basis of current world prices on the major markets for the corresponding goods. Therein, the contractual partners shall strive for a stabilization of prices."[62] Excluded from this agreement was the sugar price, which was established separately by the agreement of January 21, 1964.

Thus, there is ground to postulate that, with identical prices of imports, the terms of trade on the various types of markets varied merely through the differences in the sugar export prices. Three different international levels were determined earlier for the sugar price. If one excludes the COMECON-China market, then Cuba's true terms of trade with the nonsocialist countries were considerably less favorable than with the USSR in view of the low sugar prices.

To demonstrate the validity of this hypothesis empirically with the available data poses some problems. As a first step, a common currency denominator has to be determined for homogeneous import goods from both types of markets. On that basis, the differing prices of the import goods indicate one side of the terms of trade, while the other side is determined by the differences in the prices of homogeneous export goods for which a common denominator needs to be established.

In the case of Cuba it would seem reasonable to adopt as reference a single export commodity, since the imports were financed essentially by sugar exports alone. The differing import prices then can be transformed into reproduction costs, and the differences in costs for homogeneous import goods from the various types of markets can serve as an indication of the corresponding terms of trade. To establish these, one may proceed as follows: One determines how much sugar had to be exchanged in a given year for a specific import commodity at the free international market price. This quantity of sugar is then expressed in Cuban production costs. This is the actual reproduction price of the given product, which thus takes into consideration both sides of the particular exchange of goods. Similarly, this computation also supplies the reproduction price for the same product from the USSR. A comparison of these two figures expresses the difference between the two sets of terms of trade. If one extends this investigation to several import products, one obtains an indication of the trend in the evolution of the general terms of trade in the types of markets under scrutiny. The condition that one deal only with import products of comparable quality entails that the investigation be limited to raw materials alone. It cannot include finished industrial products which, because of varying life span, different finishings, and so forth, are not homogeneous.

Such an investigation is illustrated in table 32, in which the import prices for goods from the Western world market are determined in juxtaposition with those for the same goods from the Soviet Union, as expressed in sugar production costs and for the year 1968.[63] The selection of raw materials was limited by the condition that the USSR had to hold an import monopoly as country of origin.[64]

The results of this rather arbitrarily conceived random sampling confirm the hypothesis that the clearing prices for Soviet raw materials corresponded to the conditions obtaining on the world market. The differences chiefly are due in all probability to the fact that for the world market data f.o.b. terms were used, while in the case of the USSR c.i.f. prices were quoted, so that freight costs were included in the latter.

With respect to the Cuban exports, the price advantage with the USSR (6.11¢ per pound) over the world market (1.98¢ per pound) led to the fact that the overall terms of trade were correspondingly differentiated. Thus, the true purchasing power of the Cuban peso for staple goods in the USSR was three times as high as in the Western world. With regard to industrial goods, we remain in the realm of pure speculation. Nevertheless, it is safe to state that in view of the differentiated Cuban import requirements, no option existed with regard to a choice of the supplier market in some instances; and it is reasonable to assume that where comparable products were offered by both types of markets, the Soviet prices were in fact three times higher than those of products of Western origin. Only a divergence of such magnitude would have led to an equalization of the purchasing power of Cuban sugar on both types of markets.

The same principles may be assumed to have applied to Cuba's trading with all other socialist countries (for which similar investigations were not made in this study): Cuban sugar exports at preferential prices were compensated by imports at stabilized world market prices.

TABLE 32. Prices of Selected Cuban Import Products, Expressed in Sugar Costs, 1968

Product	Origin	Offer on Western World Market		Offer from USSR		
		Price f.o.b.[a] ($/t)	(1) Sugar Costs (Cub $/t)	Price c.i.f. (Cub $/t)	(2) Sugar Costs (Cub $/t)	(1) as % of (2)
Wheat	Canada	72.07	150.65	78.60	53.25	283
Oats	USA	48.83	79.87	74.53	50.53	158
Barley	USA	73.97	154.66	72.80	49.33	314
Corn	USA	44.88	93.81	57.28	39.00	241
Bituminous coal	USA	13.96	29.14	18.26	12.33	236
Crude oil	Venezuela	13.60	28.41	15.85	10.73	265
Aluminum	USA	564.69	1,179.94	772.70	523.34	225
Copper	USA	1,110.18	2,320.75	1,189.97	811.37	286
Sulfite cellulose	USA	132.45	276.88	125.92	85.32	325
Newsprint	USA	147.54	344.94	147.41	99.85	345

a. See Statistisches Jahrbuch für die Bundesrepublik Deutschland 1972 (Stuttgart and Mainz, 1972), appendix, pp. 98 ff.

As has been noted, these elaborations applied to 1968. Taking these data as the point of departure, the following hypotheses may be advanced for the evolution of the terms of trade on all types of markets: The exchange terms with the USSR remained constant in their general trend since Cuban sugar was compensated at fixed long-term clearing prices against imports at stabilized prices. Quite generally, the same probably applies to the remaining socialist countries, even though the terms of trade were on the average somewhat less advantageous since they paid Cuba a lower price for its sugar. However, a drastic deterioration of the Cuban terms of trade must have occurred after 1963 on the Western world market, when the sugar price sank from a high of 8.48¢ per pound to a low of 1.98¢ per pound in 1968. If import prices during that same period remained stable, the Cuban reproduction costs were bound to have more than quadrupled. However, starting with 1969, the price evolution on the sugar market underwent a reversal of this trend in favor of Cuba.

The terms of trade also include the conditions of payment. As was stated earlier, the countries of type 1 and the USSR granted credits to Cuba more or less in a proportion relative to their exports to that country. However, the other socialist countries increasingly seem to have been intent on achieving a bilateral trade balance. In absolute terms, the USSR bore by far the largest burden as creditor and granted its credits, for all intents and purposes, without interest or repayment commitment.

In addition to this overt economic aid, Cuba also received additional and sizable concealed support. It may be assumed hypothetically that the socialist countries could have bought Cuban sugar at world market prices and, if this is accepted, then the actual sugar price paid by these countries was a partial subsidy that was not offset by inflated import prices. Therefore, the subsidy contribution of the socialist countries consists of the difference between the preferential price and the world market price. The overt and concealed financing of the Cuban national economy is summarized in table 33.

Thus, it appears that in addition to the overt credits granted to cover the Cuban trade deficit and amounting to $2.6 billion between 1963 and 1970, the island also received a concealed sugar subsidy of $1.7 billion. The USSR contributed 70 percent of the overall foreign financing of the Cuban economy,[65] aid that amounted to a total of $3 billion, or a daily subvention of approximately $1 million. The participation of the remaining socialist countries amounted to 19 percent, while the balance of 11 percent was contributed by the nonsocialist countries which did not participate in subsidizing the sugar price.

A reservation is needed, however, regarding this summarized balance: In the agreement of February 13, 1960, between the USSR and Cuba, it was agreed (article 1) that 20 percent of the Cuban sugar exports were to be paid in (hard) foreign currency.[66] The sugar agreement of January 21, 1964, which formed the basis of the sugar projection plan, contained no such paragraph. If one were to assume that such a provision had remained valid until 1970, then the foreign currencies derived from the Soviet Union would have been available for financing Cuban imports from the nonsocialist market. This would have led to a shift of the credits now allocated to the Western nations to the USSR; in other words, the nonsocialist countries would not have been called upon to become Cuba's creditors.

In computing economic aid to Cuba, it was assumed also that the socialist countries in 1963 applied in their compensating accounting the average world market sugar price of 8.48¢ per pound, an assumption which surely is unrealistic. It is more plausible that Cuba, in turn, subsidized the price paid by the socialist countries for their sugar imports in that particular year.[67]

Effects of the Sugar Plan on the Domestic Economy

The priority granted to expanding the sugar economy was to have triggered an increase in the activity of corollary economic sectors in accordance with the principle of backward linkage. However, the build-up of this economic aggregate was bound to tie up labor and investment means at the expense of the rest of the economy and, therefore, to impede its full development. These three hypotheses will form the subject of the following conclusions.

Effects of the Sugar Plan on Employment

In assessing employment conditions in Cuba, one must start with the situation in the prerevolutionary period, when

TABLE 33. Financing of the Cuban National Economy by Third-Party Countries (millions of dollars)

	1963		1964		1965		1966	
	Amt.	%	Amt.	%	Amt.	%	Amt.	%
Credits								
Nonsocialist								
countries	−16	−5	34	11	53	10	70	11
USSR	297	93	135	43	105	21	247	39
COMECON and								
China	40	12	135	43	17	3	10	1
Subtotal	321	100	304	97	175	34	327	51
Subsidies								
USSR	—	—	11	3	216	43	170	27
COMECON and								
China	—	—	—	—	118	23	141	22
Subtotal	—	—	11	3	334	66	311	49
Total	321	100	315	100	509	100	638	100

Sources: Credits computed from the balances shown by Cuban trade in table 31. *Subsidies* computed on the basis of the difference between the

unemployment, particularly of a seasonal nature, constituted one of the major problems in the agrarian sector of the economy. The solutions proposed by the new government aimed at creating permanent jobs in agriculture through diversification and the extension of the sugar harvest. Nothing was done at first, however, to discourage the one-way mobility of the rural population toward the urban centers. This migration led to a growing shortage of available manpower in agriculture and, at the same time, promoted concealed underemployment in the secondary and tertiary sectors. The whole service sector, in particular, became greatly inflated as a result of the growth of the administrative and party machinery, of new mass organizations, and of the army. Unlike the Eastern European countries, the excess agricultural manpower in Cuba could not be absorbed by industry, where production only developed slowly after the revolution.[68]

The United Nations Economic Commission for Latin America

TABLE 33 (Continued)

1967		1968		1969		1970		1963–70	
Amt.	%	Amt.	%	Amt.	%	Amt.	%	Amt.	%
77	13	53	7	62	9	123	26	456	11
203	35	377	53	427	61	158	33	1,949	45
1	0	8	1	14	2	−24	−5	201	5
281	48	438	61	503	72	257	54	2,606	61
224	38	167	24	101	14	162	34	1,051	25
79	14	110	15	97	14	58	12	603	14
303	52	277	39	198	28	220	46	1,654	39
584	100	715	100	701	100	477	100	4,260	100

price for exported sugar on the socialist markets and on the world market, table 28.

(ECLA) had observed in 1965 that, generally speaking, the growth of employment in Cuba exceeded the growth of production and that, therefore, the problem of employment had been solved at the expense of the productivity of labor.[69] Castro himself confirmed the decline in work productivity:

Did the migration of rural workers to other forms of activity generate a sizeable increase in production? No. Our country is faced with the problem of a shortage of manpower. . . . In the past, we practically had to invent jobs to give some work to all those people. That is why this problem arose all of a sudden: no one ever mentioned the question of productivity as having any importance. . . . Our population has increased and yet in some classes of commodities the production is not higher but lower. . . . What is this bottomless pit which swallows up the human resources of this country . . . the wealth of this country and its material assets which we need so urgently? It is inefficiency, unproductiveness, and low productivity. Everyone in every branch of the economy is guilty of the same crime.[70]

In view of the concealed unemployment, the recruiting of harvest helpers from the cities should have been no obstacle to the expansion of the rest of the economy. Between 1964 and 1969, the same volume of sugar cane was harvested on the average as between 1951 and 1960 but over longer harvest periods and, therefore, with fewer workers. Thus, in the final result, at least the entire increase in the employable population could have been assigned to other sectors of the economy.

It was only in 1970 that a true bottleneck for the rest of the economy arose as a result of a massive recruitment of untrained harvest workers. A total of 1.2 million workers was drawn from other sectors to bring in the cane harvest,[71] so that 40 percent of the entire employable population at one time or another actively participated in the "Great *Zafra*."

It is clear that the extraordinary effort of the people not only lowered the available agricultural manpower in the non-sugar sectors to a much lower level than that averaged in any other period but also prevented . . . the workers, the students and others from the cities to engage in voluntary work . . . in other fields of endeavor independent of the *zafra*.[72]

Here is the key to the explanation of the "defeat on the second front" which was brought about by a drastic drop in the production of all other sectors of the economy.

Effects of the Sugar Plan on Investment Activities

In contrast to the first phase of the revolution, during which a rather consumption-oriented policy had been followed, accumulation was the guideline between 1964 and 1970; indeed, the rate of investment was to be increased by 30 percent by 1968.[73] Data for the allocation of investments are available only up to 1966, and these clearly reveal the shift of investment priorities to the agricultural sector.[74] In the latter, the investment budget, amounting ultimately to Cub$360 million, more than doubled between 1962 and 1966 and finally totaled half the investment volume for the entire "productive" domain. It is unlikely that this proportion changed substantially prior to 1970, since special efforts became necessary during that period in the other agrarian sectors as well, parallel to those in the sugar economy, because of the tightening of bottlenecks in food production.

In contrast, the investment shares of all other sectors decreased until 1966, with the exception of the transportation sector. This may be read as a clear sign that the increase in capital formation was achieved at the expense of industry, notwithstanding the fact that the sugar industry—as a segment of the sugar economy—was assigned statistically to the secondary area.

In summary we may conclude, therefore, that an overall shift in all investment priorities had occurred as a consequence of the sugar forecast plan and that the boost in the projected growth of the lead sector was bound to inhibit the long-term development of all other economic fields not directly connected with it.

It had been assumed from the start that capital formation in the economic branches directly linked to the sugar economy would be triggered by the expansion of the lead sector. One should keep in mind that the Cuban development strategy was determined by allowing full play to the principle of complementarity. Thus, autonomous investment in the sugar economy was to generate impulses inducing new or additional expansion investments in economic sectors interconnected with the sugar economy through their industrial ramifications. Special importance was assigned in

particular to backward linkages, while satellite industries sub-
ordinated to the lead sector were to be promoted only at a later
time. To be sure, the seven-year period under scrutiny is too short
to expect a conclusive evolution of the entire sugar net product
formation block, yet it is of interest to determine whether this
mechanism at least showed some promise of functioning as expected.

The question was examined by using as examples the development of the fertilizer and construction industries, which both are
important supply sectors, not only of the sugar economy, but of the
agrarian economy as a whole. The activities of these two branches
were monitored by analyzing the development of their production;
in the case of the construction industry, the development of the
cement industry as ancillary supplier was included in the
examination.[75]

The results showed that in industries producing primary materials, substantial capital formation had indeed taken place.[76]
However, this was not reflected in a corresponding increase in
production. The investment projects patently had been delayed
through procrastination. Though the activity of the lead sector
increased the demand for inputs, it boosted directly and primarily
import activity and led only to a very limited degree to the generation of domestic production or to its further expansion. In the
construction industry, a shift of emphasis from the building sector
in favor of civil engineering in rural areas could be observed, but it
was not accompanied by any significant increase in overall
activity.[77]

It is questionable to attempt the assessment of the activity of a
specific sector on the strength of the degree of availability of one of
its primary materials (as in the construction industry, the quantities of cement both produced and imported). But this procedure
suggests itself in the present instance because of the lack of any
better available supporting data. As in the case of the manpower
situation, the present statements regarding investment policy can
only be regarded as hypothetical conclusions, calling for more
thorough investigation.

The Evolution of the Cuban Economy as a Whole

In the attempt made here to deal with the overall evolution of Cuba's economy until 1970, it must be remembered expressly that the results are to be evaluated only to a limited extent in the light of the performance of the sugar economy. In this respect, the frame of reference of the present study already has been exceeded. Therefore, this analysis will be restricted to a summary form and will lay claim to representing merely a necessary adjunct.

For 1962 to 1968 we may refer to the official Cuban overall balance sheet for the national economy (table 34). However, caution is indicated with regard to the accuracy of the data. This summary was taken from JUCEPLAN's *Boletín Estadistico 1971,* which was published in 1973. For 1962–66, the data appearing therein are based on constant 1965 prices and had been published in *Boletín Estadistico 1968* (p. 18). The next two years are substantiated by data at current prices. It was apparently impossible to index these last data and, despite the time elapsed, they could not cover the period all the way to 1970. This seems to point to difficulties encountered by the Cuban statisticians. (Up to that point, the physical development of specific products could be corroborated in detail.)

For an understanding of the overall balance sheet of the national economy it was assumed that national income produced corresponded to the achievement level of the national economy, since it refers to the actual economic net product.[78] By adding the advance payments, the total national product is ascertained and broken down, in terms of its origin, into six economic sectors. The monetary value of the disposable national income is computed by including foreign trade and is then apportioned by utilization categories.

Cuba's produced national income increased by 18 percent between 1962 and 1968. If we leave out the advance payments, then agriculture expanded its share at the expense of industry, the production of which showed the slowest rate of development among all the net product areas.

The share of exports in produced national income decreased

TABLE 34. Balance Sheet of the Cuban National Economy
(million Cuban pesos)

	1962[a]		1963[a]		1964[a]	
	Amt.	Index	Amt.	Index	Amt.	Index
National product						
Agriculture	941	100	904	96	959	102
Industry	2,746	100	2,701	98	2,814	102
Construction	370	100	348	94	422	114
Transportation	290	100	298	103	340	117
Communication	45	100	48	107	49	109
Trade	1,690	100	1,714	101	1,871	110
Total	6,082	100	6,013	99	6,455	106
Advance payments	2,384	100	2,276	96	2,379	100
Produced						
national income	3,698	100	3,737	101	4,076	110
Plus imports	783	100	769	98	991	127
Minus exports	688	100	476	69	568	82
Disposable national income	3,793	100	4,030	106	4,499	119
Private Consumption	2,491	100	2,653	107	2,781	112
Collective Consumption	417	100	397	95	489	117
Total consumption	2,908	100	3,050	105	3,269	112
Investments	626	100	733	117	810	129
Changes in Inventories	259	100	247	96	419	162
Accumulation	885	100	980	111	1,229	139

Source: JUCEPLAN, *Boletín Estadistico 1971* (Havana, n.d.), p. 44.
a. In 1965 prices.
b. In current prices.

TABLE 34 (Continued)

1965[a]		1966[a]		1967[b]		1968[b]	
Amt.	Index	Amt.	Index	Amt.	Index	Amt.	Index
1,074	114	1,042	111	1,120	119	1,352	144
2,913	106	2,859	104	3,185	116	3,130	114
522	141	518	140	598	162	526	142
348	120	373	129	385	133	611	211
52	116	56	124	57	124	60	133
1,862	110	1,865	110	1,867	111	1,652	98
6,771	111	6,709	110	7,212	119	7,331	121
2,633	110	2,725	114	3,129	131	2,978	125
4,138	112	3,986	108	4,083	110	4,353	118
886	113	894	114	994	127	1,113	142
713	103	586	85	747	108	685	99
4,311	114	4,294	113	4,330	114	4,781	126
2,888	116	2,772	111	2,678	108	3,298	132
474	114	474	114	517	t24	490	118
3,363	116	3246	112	3,195	110	3,788	130
842	135	935	149	1,032	165	918	147
107	41	113	44	103	40	75	29
949	107	1,048	118	1,135	128	993	112

from 19 to 13 percent, while the share of imports in the disposable national income dropped from 26 to 23 percent. Even though the statistics seem to indicate that in this instance the national economy became more independent of foreign trade, one must keep in mind that the sugar plan aimed at achieving a growing interdependence in foreign trade relations. The stagnation in exports was due almost exclusively to the nonfulfillment of the sugar plan. As a result of the growing net imports, the disposable national income increased by 25 percent, illustrating the prominent contribution of the Soviet Union to the development of the Cuban economy.

The investment rate, in relation to the disposable national income, rose from 16 to 26 percent (1967) but could not be held at that level the following year. The result was that consumption (1967) only increased by 10 percent and, at the same time, on a per capita basis remained below the level of 1962.[79]

Taken together, these data permit the conclusion that domestic demand increased slightly up to 1968 but that, at the same time, imports rose faster than domestic production.

For 1969 and 1970, we are restricted in our considerations to the physical evolution of specific products. What becomes abundantly clear is that in 1970 the whole economy suffered a serious setback. As early as July 26, 1970, Castro intimated such a development:

I repeat that we proved unable to win what we called the simultaneous battle. . . . The heroic effort to raise our production, to raise our purchasing potential, led to a disruption of the economy, to a setback in production in other sectors, and ultimately to a multiplication of our problems.[80]

Hardest hit were agriculture and industry. Thus, for instance, dairy production declined below the absolute level of 1963,[81] although, next to the sugar economy, the promotion of the cattle industry had been given special attention. The production of fruit in 1969 and 1970 dropped 25 percent below that of 1968, and a decrease was also noted in vegetable crops. Serious setbacks were recorded in the industrial sector as well, particularly in the production of consumer goods, but also in the production of intermediary goods, such as cement and fertilizers.

The immediate consequence of the drop in production and of the bottlenecks in the distribution system was an ever more stringent belt-tightening for the Cuban population. Furthermore, the diminution in the offer of available goods no longer could be neutralized by redistribution measures. With the exception of the top officials, no groups were left whose consumption could have been curtailed any further. Moreover, the relatively high share in the overall consumption of collective usufruct, that is, services subsumed under the concept of indirect income, leads to the conclusion that the distribution of the available end product already was relatively uniform.

The revolutionary government's attempt to ensure that everyone be provided with the material necessities despite the worsening economic situation ultimately safeguarded what otherwise easily could have been lost as a result of the expansionary economic policies: the very economic survival of the revolution per se as the irreducible minimum goal. That even this goal could be achieved only through massive aid from the USSR does not speak well for the economic policies pursued by Cuba up to 1970.

An attempt to analyze the causes of the unsatisfactory evolution in the production sector would constitute a separate subject for investigation which is only partially covered by examination of Cuban sugar policy. Insofar as conjectures suggest themselves for the other economic sectors, they all point to the assumption that the inhibiting factors were similar to those in the sugar economy. In foreign trade the key factor, in my opinion, was not so much the severely curtailed import capability, since industrial installations and technical know-how continued to be supplied. The problem of spare parts, resulting from the embargo by the United States and the concomitant overtaxing of the existing facilities, affected all branches of the economy. Beyond that, however, and of decisive importance, was the political regulatory machinery. On the one hand, it gave rise to excessive bureaucratization and, on the other hand and contrary to the hopes of Guevara, it had a detrimental effect on the work morale of the population. Both led to organizational and implementational shortcomings within the production sector. To be sure, such difficulties can be accounted for by the drastic social transformation then in progress; yet this very process was directed by the highest leadership of the nation, which failed to hold together what still could have been an efficiently operating production system. In view of the strongly centralized organization structure and a one-way information flow from the top downward, the responsibility for these shortcomings also is to be placed squarely at the top.

The consequences for the Cuban leadership were manifest. Little objection could be raised to the operational aspect of the policy strategy; after all, sugar was still the commodity which the country was able to produce traditionally and at advantageous costs. The continuous increase in the price of sugar on the free international market has already multiplied Cuban foreign currency revenue in the 1970s and has improved the terms of trade for Cuba considerably. It may be assumed that the Soviet Union will adapt its conditions to this rise in price, since otherwise Cuba would see advantages in an increased economic rapprochement with the Western industrial nations.

It became clear, though, that the foremost requirement was to set a growth rhythm in sugar production which would obviate a repetition of the external costs which were a burden in 1970. The concept of backward linkage also could be preserved, since the continued priority given to sugar production obviously called for substantial improvements in the obsolete processing technology. This concept heretofore had not failed to stimulate the inception of a precursory ancillary industry, and if it had not yet had its full effect, this was only because of the stagnation of the lead sector.

An urgent need for a change in course seemed indicated, however, with regard to regulatory policies. Such a shift was introduced after 1970, chiefly by a renewed emphasis on operational profitability and an increase in the use of material incentives which were accompanied by an ideological shift toward the Soviet doctrine of the day.[82] Moreover, Cuba in 1975 was to receive a constitution which may incorporate experiences, hitherto tested only on the regional level, of far-ranging participation in the decision-making process.

Finally, I will hazard a glance into the future. A development strategy which, in relation to that of 1963 to 1970, will contain only minor changes, should form a sound basis for a successful policy of accumulation in view of substantially improved sales conditions for sugar on the world market. But, in addition, safeguards must be provided for the framework of regulatory policies to correspond better to the requirements of economic efficiency. Concentrated attention is being focused in Cuba on this problem at the very moment of writing the present study. The fruits of these efforts could appear by 1980 in that Cuba by then may have decisively outdistanced the other countries of Latin America in providing material goods to its population and may have found at the same time a workable link to the industrial nations.

NOTES
BIBLIOGRAPHY
INDEX

Notes

Chapter 1. Development Strategy

1. I shall forgo a detailed outline of Cuban development policy between 1959 and 1963, since the topic has been surveyed in depth by other authors. I recommend Edward Boorstein, *The Economic Transformation of Cuba* (New York: Monthly Review Press, 1968); René Dumont, *Cuba: Socialisme et développement* (Paris, 1964); James O'Connor, *Origins of Socialism in Cuba* (Ithaca: Cornell University Press, 1970); Dudley Seers, ed., *Cuba: The Economic and Social Revolution* (Chapel Hill: University of North Carolina Press, 1964); and with reservations Robin Blackburn, "The Economics of the Cuban Revolution," in *Latin America and the Caribbean*, ed. Claudio Veliz (New York: Praeger, 1968), pp. 622–31; Theodore Draper, *Castroism, Theory and Practice* (New York: Praeger, 1969); Leo Huberman and Paul Sweezy, *Socialism in Cuba* (New York: Monthly Review Press, 1969); and Carmelo Mesa-Lago, "Economic Policies and Growth," in *Revolutionary Change in Cuba*, ed. idem (Pittsburgh: University of Pittsburgh Press, 1971), pp. 277–338. For agriculture specifically, see the excellent contribution of Michel Gutelman, *L'Agriculture socialisée à Cuba* (Paris, 1967).

Benjamin Higgins, in *Economic Development: Problems, Principles and Policies*, 2d ed. (New York: Norton, 1968), has compiled general characteristics of underdevelopment which are useful for an empirical investigation (pp. 16 ff.). On the basis of the criteria mentioned, he classifies Cuba before the revolution among the underdeveloped countries (pp. 792–93).

2. The population figure is for 1958. See Paul Roberts, ed., *Cuba 1968* (Los Angeles; University of California Latin American Center, 1970), p. 12.

3. See O'Connor, who attempts to give empirical proof (*Origins of Socialism*, pp. 33 ff.).

4. The statistical data on Cuban sugar production are quoted from International Sugar Council, ed., *The World Sugar Economy: Structure and Policies*, vol. 1, *National Sugar Economies and Policies* (London, 1963), pp. 126 ff.; and JUCEPLAN, *Boletín Estadístico 1970* (Havana, n.d.), p. 136.

5. See State of Hawaii, Department of Planning and Economic Development, *The Sugar Industry in Hawaii* (Honolulu, 1973), p. 17.

6. See also Boorstein's explanations, *Economic Transformation*, p. 4.

7. See O'Connor, *Origins of Socialism*, pp. 59 ff.

8. The structure and development of the sugar economy are studied here in greater detail than might appear appropriate so that basic facts, essential to the formulation of marketing policy for Cuban sugar after the revolution, can be included.

9. In the present case, opportunity costs arise when, because of lower production costs for imported sugar, a decrease in revenue can be foreseen. It would be of interest to know, however, whether relative cost differentials for cane and beets can be determined. To the best of my knowledge, such a comparison has been made to date only by Ford Sturrock ("Sugar Beet or Sugar Cane?", *Journal of Agricultural Economics,* 20, no. 1 [1969]) and did not lead to an unequivocal general conclusion.

10. See International Sugar Council, ed., *The World Sugar Economy: Structure and Policies,* vol. 2, *The World Picture* (1963), p. 91.

11. *Sugar yield* is defined as the ratio between raw sugar produced and agricultural area; *agricultural yield* is the ratio between sugar cane or sugar beet and the agricultural area; *industrial yield* is the ratio between raw sugar produced and sugar cane or sugar beet processed. Throughout, I have treated Hawaii as separate from the United States unless otherwise noted.

12. The FAO, for example, uses this upper limit. See FAO, *Agricultural Commodities Projections, 1970–1980* (Rome, 1971), vol. 2.

13. See A. Viton and F. Pignalosa, *Trends and Forces in World Sugar Consumption,* FAO Commodity Bulletin Series, no. 32 (Rome, 1961), p. 36.

14. It is obvious that where nominal per capita income is high, quantity demand will react less to a price change than would be the case with lower income. Conversely, at a high price, income elasticity of demand is less than at a low price.

15. *World Sugar Economy,* vol. 2, p. 122.

16. The far-reaching restructuring of the sugar trade, in connection with the reorientation of Cuban sugar exports to the socialist countries and the resulting (provisional) distribution of Cuba's U.S. sugar quota among other exporting countries, has been studied in depth by Gerhard Hagelberg, "Strukturwandlungen in der Weltzuckerwirtschaft seit 1960," in *Jahrbuch für Wirtschaftsgeschichte 1969/IV* (Berlin, GDR, 1969), pp. 99 ff.

17. A detailed discussion of preferential sugar markets until 1961 appears in *World Sugar Economy,* vol. 2, pp. 165 ff., which may be considered the standard work. I shall therefore confine myself to a summary.

18. See *World Sugar Economy,* vol. 1, p. 78.

19. According to an FAO projection (*Agricultural Commodities Projections,* vol. 2, p. 7).

20. The International Sugar Council defined the free sugar market as a type of market where that portion of the sugar supply was traded which remained after deducting from the total trade volume all "internal" exports (for example, Hawaii–United States) and those between dependent territories and mother countries, as well as all other U.S. imports and the quantities imported by the Soviet Union from other socialist countries (*World Sugar Economy,* vol. 2, pp. 212–13).

Thus, in spite of their discriminatory nature, all the other cartels belonged by definition to the free market. This meant that the free market laid claim to a much larger portion of the total turnover than the raw sugar actually offered on a short-term basis, which was the determining factor in pricing. This, together with the fact that Cuba had hardly any refined sugar to offer, brought about the need for a better definition.

21. This definition was offered by Maryanna Boynton, "Effects of Embargo and Boycott: The Cuban Case" (Ph.D. dissertation, University of California at Riverside, 1972).

22. The Soviet Union purchased from Cuba 462,000 tons of raw sugar in 1955 and 351,000 tons in 1957 (International Sugar Council, ed., *Sugar Yearbook 1960* [London, 1961], p. 168).

23. See, above all, Andres Bianchi, "Agriculture," in *Cuba: The Economic and Social Revolution,* ed. Dudley Seers, pp. 65–157.

24. See Dudley Seers, "The Economic and Social Background," in his *Cuba: The Economic and Social Revolution,* pp. 3–61.

25. See United States Sugar Act of 1948, quoted in *Anuario Azucarero de Cuba 1962* (Havana, 1964), p. 7, sec. 207(e)(1): "None of the proration established for Cuba may be filled by direct consumption sugar."

26. Max Nolff, "Industry," in *Cuba: The Economic and Social Revolution,* ed. Dudley Seers, pp. 283–338.

27. UNESCO estimated the proportion of middle and higher income groups in Cuba before the revolution at 22 percent of the total population. Income differences existed mainly between the urban and rural populations (Draper, *Castroism,* pp. 78–79; and Higgins, *Economic Development,* p. 790).

28. The open and concealed unemployment which was unquestionably one of Cuba's major problems before the revolution is still being discussed today because of its extent. Analyses by O'Connor (*Origins of Socialism,* pp. 328 ff.) and Mesa-Lago ("Economic Policies and Growth," pp. 277 ff.) are available. I have used here Castro's statement from his first speech, "Historia me absolverá," in 1953.

29. Mesa-Lago, "Economic Policies and Growth," p. 277, summarizes Cuba's socioeconomic problems before the revolution as follows: "(a) the relatively small rate of economic growth, (b) the excessive significance of sugar in the generation of GNP and exports, (c) the overwhelming dependence on the United States in regard to capital and trade, (d) the high rates of unemployment and underemployment, and (e) the wide differences in standards of living between urban and rural areas." All these symptoms are mentioned with varying emphasis in the literature (see chap. 1, n. 1). Draper (*Castroism,* pp. 97 ff.) nevertheless is not reconciled to the concept of "underdevelopment" in Cuba's case.

30. The per capita GNP was $402 in 1958 (Carmelo Mesa-Lago, *Availability and Reliability of Statistics in Socialist Cuba,* 2d ed. [University of Pittsburgh, Center for Latin American Studies, 1970], pp. 48, 52).

31. O'Connor, *Origins of Socialism,* pp. 3 ff., divides the interpretation of the Cuban revolution by its numerous critics into two schools of thought. The first,

predominantly more moderate, going all the way to revanchist convictions, starts from the premise that Castro pushed the revolution beyond the stage of reforms called for by the system, and thus betrayed it. Draper can be considered an advocate of this school, though a very prudent and circumspect one. The other side, which deals with the causes of social imbalance and the legitimacy of the socialist revolution under the catchword "imperialism," is headed by Boorstein.

Both schools have in common the invocation of essentially subjective factors as the determinants of the course of the revolution—in one case Castro's radicalism, in the other the counterrevolutionary activities of the United States. O'Connor himself follows a third direction by attempting to prove that Cuba's socialist development was inherent in the historical (objective) position of the country and consequently inevitable.

32. Since it cannot be the object of the present study to take part in this discussion, I have followed the pragmatic and undoubtedly simpler course of examining how Cuba's revolutionary movement itself interpreted the facts and the conclusions it drew.

33. On July 26, 1953, a small group attempted an armed uprising against the Batista dictatorship. The Castro brothers survived, and in court Fidel developed the basic postulates of the later rebels in his first known speech, "La historia me absolverá." In the years before 1959, the "Manifiesto de la Sierra Maestra," which contained socioeconomic propositions, gained greater importance. Draper, (*Castroism*, p. 12) has compiled the different programs of the "26th of July Movement," evaluated them, and confronted them with later measures of the revolutionary government.

34. Ibid., pp. 4 ff.

35. "Una estrategía de desarrollo orientada a transformar radicalmente la dependencia política y económica prerevolucionaria aún prevalesciente, para lograr independencia e igualdad en las relaciones internacionales" ("La estrategía de desarrollo económico, informe presentado por la delagación cubana al Tercer Seminario Interregional sobre Planificación del Desarrollo, Santiago de Chile, marzo 1968," quoted in David Barkin, "Agricultura: El sector clave del desarrollo de Cuba," *Economía y Desarrollo*, no. 3 (July–September 1970):45.

36. See Paul Baran, *The Political Economy of Growth* (New York: Monthly Review Press, 1957); and André Gunder Frank, *Capitalism and Underdevelopment in Latin America* (New York: Monthly Review Press, 1969). Frank is the actual founder of the "*dependencia*" theory, which has found ready acceptance— especially in Latin America—but is now being modified.

37. For further details about the first land reform, see Gutelman, *L'Agriculture socialisée*, pp. 151 ff.; Jacques Chonchol, "Analisis crítico de la reforma agraria cubana," *El Trimestre Económico*, 30, no. 117 (January–March 1963):69–143; and Dumont, *Cuba: Socialisme et développement*, pp. 35 ff.

38. See Dumont, *Cuba: Socialisme et développement*, pp. 55 ff., and idem, *Cuba est-il socialiste?* (Paris, 1970), pp. 43–44.

39. Boorstein, *Economic Transformation*, pp. 135 ff., 160.

40. "There is a danger of not seeing the forest because of the trees. Pursuing the

chimera of achieving socialism with the aid of the blunted weapons left to us by capitalism (the commodity as the economic cell, profitability, and individual material interest as levers, etc.), it is possible to come to a blind alley. And the arrival there comes about after covering a long distance where there are many crossroads and where it is difficult to realize just when the wrong turn was taken. Meanwhile, the adapted economic base has undermined the development of consciousness. To build communism, a new man must be created simultaneously with the material base" (Ernesto Che Guevara, "Man and Socialism in Cuba," in *Man and Socialism in Cuba,* ed. Bertram Silverman [New York: Atheneum, 1971], pp. 342–43).

Guevara considered the retention of the so-called system of material incentives particularly harmful (although a temporarily necessary evil), as it would undermine the development of the "new morality": "For advocates of financial self-management, the use of direct material incentives throughout the various stages of building communism does not contradict the 'development' of consciousness. But for us it does. It is for this reason that we struggle against the predominance of material incentives—because they would retard the development of socialist morality" ("On the Budgetary Finance System," ibid., p. 134).

Under the system of "material incentives" meant for the primary and tertiary sectors, the production units were to remain relatively autonomous within the framework of a decentralized planning model and were to adjust their activities to the market. Guevara, however, defined his proposed model as follows:

> The most immediate difference arises with regard to the enterprise. For us, an enterprise is a conglomerate of factories or production units that use similar technologies, possess a common market for their output, or are located, in some cases, in the same geographical area. The economic calculus system views an enterprise as a production unit with its own legal personality. . . . Another difference is the way money is used. Under our system, it functions only as a means of measurement, a price reflection of enterprise performance that is analyzed by central administrative bodies so as to be able to control such performance. . . . Consequently, because of the way in which money is used, our enterprises have no funds of their own. There are separate bank accounts for withdrawals and deposits . . . all deposits come automatically under State control. . . .
>
> The budgetary system is based on centralized control of the enterprise's activity. Its plan and economic activity are directly controlled by central administrative bodies; it has no funds of its own nor does it receive bank credits. And it uses material incentives on an individual basis or, in other words, individual monetary premiums or penalties. At the proper time, it will also institute collective incentives. Direct material incentives, however, are limited by the method of wage payment." (ibid., pp. 132 ff.)

41. Albán Lataste, *Cuba: ¿ hacia una nueva economía política del socialismo?* (Santiago de Chile, 1968), p. 45. Although he is Chilean, Lataste was Cuban deputy secretary for planning in 1966.

42. Ibid., p. 36; and Dumont, *Cuba: Socialisme et développement,* pp. 55 ff. and 65 ff.

43. Regino Botî, "El plan de desarrollo económico de 1962," *Cuba Socialista,* 1, no. 4 (December 1961):19.

44. According to Botî, the following objectives were to be reached (they are quoted here only to show more clearly the excessive optimism of the early revolutionary phase): "First in America in per capita production of steel, cement, electrical power and, with the exception of Venezuela, in oil refining; First in Latin America in tractors and textiles . . . ; Second in the world in nickel output" (ibid., p. 31).

45. Boynton made this statement and substantiated it very carefully ("Effects of Embargo and Boycott," p. 41).

46. According to Blackburn, the Soviet Union by 1963 had delivered more than sixty industrial plants to Cuba ("Economics of the Cuban Revolution," p. 627).

47. ECLA, *Economic Survey of Latin America, 1963* (New York, 1965), pp. 267–68.

48. Dumont, *Cuba: Socialisme et développement,* pp. 70–71.

49. FAO, *Monthly Bulletin of Agricultural Economics and Statistics,* 19 (July–August 1970):14–17, cited in Mesa-Lago, "Economic Policies and Growth," p. 329.

50. Carlos Romeo, "Acerca del desarrollo económica de Cuba," *Cuba Socialista,* 5, no. 52 (December 1965):2–24.

51. Ibid.

52. "La experiencia de Cuba en comercio exterior," *Comercio Exterior* (April–June 1964):110 ff.

53. Mesa-Lago, "Economic Policies and Growth," p. 290.

54. Detlef Lorenz has described systematically the significance for developing countries of being tied to the world economy ("Zur Typologie der Entwicklungsländer," in *Entwicklungsländer,* ed. Bruno Fritsch (Cologne and Berlin, 1968), pp. 46 ff.

55. Albert Hirschman, *The Strategy of Economic Development* (New Haven: Yale University Press, 1958).

I do not want to give the impression that the Cubans followed Hirschman to the letter. He is mentioned merely because his conclusions concerning a small country with limited resources and domestic markets largely coincide with the Cuban growth model. According to Romeo ("Acerca del desarrollo," pp. 11–12), the latter was derived and further developed from the Marxist model of expanded reproduction: "It is well known that this theory [of classic socialist economic development] is based on Marx's reproduction model from which the necessity of proportionate development . . . of the whole economy . . . may be deduced." This in turn leads to the priority given to the development of producers' goods industries in order to accelerate the growth of the economy, or of the productivity of labor. "Traditionally, this dynamic model is tailored to a closed economy and assigns second place to foreign trade. This description is indeed in accordance with

Soviet experience. . . . If this traditional model is applied to Cuba's particular conditions, it becomes immediately apparent that within the reproduction, foreign trade, on the contrary, plays a leading role and not a secondary one. This makes it necessary to start from a reproduction which is not based on the domestic production [as in a closed system], but includes explicitly . . . foreign trade in the manner of an open system.'' Under this assumption, production of industrial goods could be ensured practically through production of primary goods, provided there is a "fair value" exchange of goods. In this respect, we may quote Baran: "In that case export industries, regardless of the physical nature of their output, become 'producers' goods' industries since their product—foreign exchange—can be converted into capital goods. Whether such a course is advisable depends on the natural resources of the country in question, on the comparative possibilities of productivity increases in producers' goods industries and those working for export, as well as on the terms of trade which the developing country may expect to face after the expansion of its exports'' (*Political Economy of Growth,* pp. 284–85).

It is interesting that the conditions mentioned by Baran appear to be fulfilled in a positive sense for the Cuban economy. This would explain why "an 'outward directed' economic development proved practicable.'' In this light, the two typical sets of problems of export-oriented economies—stable prices and stable markets—can be regarded as having been solved by Cuba's integration into the trade system of the socialist countries. The problem of determining the lead sector ("del desarollo preferente del sector exportador'') may be solved by taking the following criteria into account: considerations of division of labor on an international level, of technology, and of complementarity. On this last point, Romeo says: "It should not be forgotten that an export item, before it reaches the world market, undergoes a series of production processes. The sugar economy is a typical example. In the same manner, exports of meat, dairy products, or fruit presuppose a processing industry. . . . To summarize, the question is not to create an export industry in the colonial or neocolonial sense, but to open up a set ("centro de actividades'') of production opportunities which, on the basis of international equivalent technology, are rooted in the domestic economy because they require complementarity which, thanks to the [broad supply structure of the socialist] foreign markets, can likewise be integrated by applying modern technology.'' At the same time, export expansion, which also stimulates imports, encourages in the long run substitution of selected imports. A typical example would be the possibility of developing a modern fertilizer industry to supply modernized export-oriented agriculture.

To be sure, the growth of the export economy would remain tied to the development of demand in the socialist world market, but in this connection, it may be pointed out that the latter grew even faster between 1956 and 1963 than the national economies concerned.

If we set aside the diverging premises of "bourgeois" and Marxist growth theory, I believe that the principal elements of Hirschman's and Cuba's strategies for a small country are in agreement (even the so-called linkage effects are based on complementary production).

56. See, for instance, "Sugar Policy and the Long-Run Orientation of the Economy," in Boorstein, *Economic Transformation*, pp. 181 ff.

57. Only the relative production cost of sugar was economically relevant for the Soviet Union. Dumont mentions that in the Ukraine sugar costs are twice as high as in Cuba, but he gives no figures (*Cuba: Socialisme et développement*, p. 126).

58. These are the words of Romeo, who does not define the basis on which the valuation was to be made ("Acerca del desarrollo," p. 14).

59. See Boorstein, *Economic Transformation*, p. 204.

Chapter 2. Economic Planning

1. The model of Cuba's economic overall planning is described in detail in JUCEPLAN, "La planificación económica en Cuba," in *Aspectos administrativos de la planificación: Documentos de un seminario* (Havana, n.d.).

2. Tomás Martinez mentions, though, that as early as 1963 there existed in Cuba "planning directives which were the basis of the formulation of a sugar plan with a goal of 10 million tons annually by 1970" ("New Goals in the Development of the Cuban Sugar Industry," *CubaAzúcar* [May–July 1967]:40). Thus, a production plan was at least mentioned, though only its overall yearly target figures were made public.

3. Hirschmüller, on the occasion of his visit to Cuba, was told of the following actions taken to reach 10 million tons: "increase of the cultivated area by 50 percent; increase of the [agricultural] yield by 25 percent" (H. Hirschmüller and H. J. Delavier, "Vor der grossen Zafra. Die Zuckerwirtschaft Kubas 10 Jahre nach der Revolution," in *Zeitschrift für Zuckerindustrie*, 1969 [Berlin, 1969], installment 2, p. 7).

Martinez gives as the 1970 goal production of 84 million tons of sugar cane on an agricultural area of over 1.6 million hectares ("New Goals," p. 40). This corresponds for 1970 to an industrial yield of 12 percent; an agricultural yield of 56 tons per hectare; and to the following 1964 base values: an agricultural yield of 45 tons per hectare; a cultivated area of 1 million hectares; cane production of 45 million tons; and, with an industrial yield of 12.5 percent, to an end product of 5.6 million tons of raw sugar.

4. Since the *zafra* does not last all year, the harvest season is a determining factor for the input of the primary factors mentioned. If for a given production goal the harvest season is shortened, a correspondingly greater daily processing capacity has to be provided, and the daily manpower requirement also increases.

5. For further details, see Hirschmüller and Delavier, "Vor der grossen Zafra," p. 2.

6. See *World Sugar Economy*, vol. 1, p. 125. In 1962 the industrial capacity was 553,000 tons per day. To what extent sugar mills had been cannibalized in the meantime cannot be ascertained exactly. It may be assumed that they were in poor condition because of the spare parts problem in the wake of the U.S. embargo.

7. According to Hirschmüller and Delavier, "Vor der grossen Zafra," p. 4.

8. According to Castro, in 1970 Cuba was to process the 84 million tons of sugar cane over an (extended) harvest period of 217 days with a projected (reduced) capacity of 620,000 tons (speech of October 27, 1969). This corresponds to an average of 387,000 tons of sugar processed per day, or a utilization of 63 percent. Chapter 3 will show to what extent we are dealing with figures actually realized.

9. For the sake of expediency, we must assume that the harvest period is the quotient of the total sugar cane production and the technically determined daily production. This leads to the fictional premise that the harvest on the first day of the *zafra* is as big as during the peak period, which distorts the real picture.

10. The average productivity of labor has been calculated with the help of two sources. First, it was important to know the number of field hands at any given moment. Castro indicated that a total of 350,000 people were to participate in the cane harvest in March 1970 (speech of October 27, 1969). If the harvest volume at this period is known, the productivity of labor can be calculated. The sugar plan (published daily in the central organ of the PCC, *Granma*) anticipated a raw sugar production of 2 million tons between February 28 and April 3, 1970. Using the peak industrial yield of 12.5 percent, production of 16 million tons of sugar cane was needed. This comes to 533,000 tons a day for the 30 actual working days, and if you divide by the number of workers mentioned, the performance rate is 1.522 tons. This referred to the whole harvesting process—cutting, cleaning, loading, and transporting the cane to the mill. The cutting itself absorbed 66 percent of the labor force.

This result, too, was extracted from Castro's speech of October 27, 1969. The empirical rate with regard to the daily average performance amounted to 2.3 tons, so that in March 1970, 233,000 *macheteros,* that is, 66 percent of all field workers, must have been used. It is not known on what assumption Castro based his proclamation.

11. See pp. 44–45.

12. JUCEPLAN, *Boletín Estadístico 1970,* p. 136.

13. See pp. 46–47.

14. Hirschmüller and Delavier's statement has been corrected by 1 percent for the sake of consistency ("Vor der grossen Zafra," p. 7).

15. Hirschmüller and Delavier indicate as further measures "increase of the effective duration of the campaign by 55 percent, expansion of plant capacity by 22 percent to 670,000 tons per day" (ibid., pp. 4, 7). See also Martinez, "New Goals," p. 49.

16. Speech of October 27, 1969.

17. See pp. 66–73.

18. Boorstein, *Economic Transformation,* pp. 187 ff.

19. FAO, "Agricultural Commodities Projections for 1970," Special Supplement to *FAO Commodity Review 1962* (Rome, 1962), pp. II-32 ff.

20. Ibid., pp. I-3–I-4.

21. Ibid., p. II-35.

22. See table 26.

23. FAO, "Agricultural Commodities Projections," p. II-37.

24. FAO estimated the population of China at 848 million (*Agricultural Commodities Projections 1970–1980,* vol. 2, p. 7). This is not the place to inquire into the reliability of this figure. I have based my statement on a population of half a billion.

25. The Soviet Union and Cuba:

> considering that sugar production is a basic branch of the Republic of Cuba's economy, and for the purpose of assisting the planned development of the socialist economy of the Republic of Cuba,
>
> despite the fact, that the Soviet Union is capable of producing a sufficient amount of sugar to meet the demands of her population and for export, nevertheless, bearing in mind the existing relations of fraternal friendship between the Soviet Union and the Republic of Cuba, and
>
> proceeding from the principle of international socialist division of labor and the advantages derived from the correct application of this principle in the interest of both countries, have agreed to the following:
>
> *Art. 1.* The Soviet Union will purchase raw sugar in the Republic of Cuba during the years 1965–1970 in the following annual amounts: 2,100,000 tons in 1965; 3,000,000 tons in 1966; 4,000,000 tons in 1967; 5,000,000 tons in 1968; 5,000,000 tons in 1969; and 5,000,000 tons in 1970.
>
> The sugar will be paid for under the terms of existing trade agreements between the USSR and the Republic of Cuba through deliveries to the Republic of Cuba of Soviet goods required by it.
>
> *Art. 2.* For purposes of removing the influence of conjunctural fluctuations of world market prices on the economy of the Republic of Cuba and to create a firm base for planning the development of the Republic of Cuba's economy over a prolonged period, both sides have agreed to establish a permanent price for the raw sugar delivered from the Republic of Cuba to the USSR through the 1965–1970 period, amounting to six American cents per pound f.a.s. at Cuban ports. (*Current Digest of the Soviet Press,* 5, no. 4 [1964], p. 27)

Boorstein mentions 6.11¢ per pound for the USSR and China (*Economic Transformation,* p. 209), as does Castro in retrospect (speech of May 20, 1970). Consequently, I have used this price as the computation basis instead of only 6¢ per pound.

26. Speech of October 31, 1964.

27. Hirschmüller and Delavier, "Vor der grossen Zafra," p. 7.

28. Armando Betancourt, "Study in Extraneous Matter in Sugar Cane," *CubaAzúcar* (September–December 1966):80 ff.

29. See pp. 87–89.

30. It is not my intention to give the impression that certain cost factors (excessively low sugar cane costs) not taken into account counterbalance exactly the

processing costs (which are too high). We are dealing here merely with counteracting trends.

31. Gutelman, *L'Agriculture socialisée*, p. 204.

32. "Lamborn's Chart of World Sugar Prices 1931–1971," in *Sugar Manual 1972*, ed. Hawaiian Sugar Planter's Association (Honolulu, 1972), p. 32.

33. In this context, quotient from net revenues (difference between export costs and gross export revenue) and gross export revenue (total amount of export sales).

34. Until 1970, the Cuban peso (Cub$), although nonconvertible, was pegged officially at the value of the U.S. dollar.

35. See pp. 120–25.

36. Assuming a world market price of only 2.75¢ per pound.

37. According to Gutelman, the overall investment for the Five-Year Plan was set by the Ministry for Sugar Economy at Cub$1.02 billion (1965) (*L'Agriculture socialisée*, p. 207). Two years later Martinez cited an amount of Cub$800 million ("New Goals," p. 42). Rodriguez further reduced this figure to Cub$400 million (Carlos Rafael Rodriguez, "Informe de la Delegación Cubana al XV período de sesiones de la Conferencia de la FAO, Roma 1969," *Economía y Desarrollo,* 1 [January–March 1970]:28). In my opinion, this reduction merely reflected the foreign currency shortage manifested during the implementation of the plan.

38. Martinez, "New Goals," p. 50.

39. Ibid., p. 50.

40. According to *Noticias Económicas,* 5, no. 40 (Havana, 1969):3.

41. Hawaii, *Sugar Industry in Hawaii,* p. 17.

42. Computed from data on pp. 24 and 35 of J. A. Mollett, "Capital in Hawaiian Sugar: Its Formation and Relation to Labor and Output, 1870–1957," *Agricultural Economics Bulletin* (Honolulu, June 1961). The proceeds per ton of sugar in 1957 amounted to $127.28. The capital input in the field accordingly amounted to 0.16 x 127.28=$20.36 per ton. Understandably, this figure can be transposed to the prerevolutionary Cuban sugar economy only with many reservations, but it may serve here as a clue to the situation.

43. Martinez, "New Goals," p. 45.

44. Armando Betancourt, "Harvest Mechanization and Its Effects on Cane Quality," *CubaAzúcar* (July–September 1970):45. He mentions capacities of 800 to 1,200 tons.

45. Capacity data from Betancourt, ibid., p. 94; number of harvesting combines from Martinez, "New Goals," p. 45.

46. Martinez, "New Goals," p. 45.

47. Ibid., p. 49.

48. Ibid., p. 43.

49. Ibid., pp. 44 ff.

50. Hirschmüller and Delavier, "Vor der grossen Zafra," p. 2.

51. Based on parity between the dollar and the Cuban peso which Castro postulated for computation purposes. See pp. 120–25.

Chapter 3. Implementation of the Development Strategy

1. This actually refers to the harvest year 1963–64, since the "little *zafra*" usually takes place during December of the preceding year and is then added to the "big *zafra*" which lasts until May or June.

2. JUCEPLAN, *Boletín Estadístico 1970*, p. 48. These data are for the entire duration of the plan. *Cana planta*, the newly planted sugar cane, in contrast to "stubble cane," has higher agricultural and industrial yields.

3. Castro, speech of October 10, 1964.

4. According to Castro (speech of December 7, 1970), the number of professional cane cutters (*macheteros*) sank from 350,000 before the revolution to 143,000 in 1967, and to 80,000 by the end of 1970.

5. Castro, speech of October 10, 1964.

6. Castro, speech of January 2, 1964. As a result of the high sugar price, Cuba expected satisfactory export revenues.

7. The quantitative data on Cuban exports, divided into regional markets and covering 1964–70, were derived exclusively from International Sugar Organization, *Sugar Yearbook 1970* (London, 1971), pp. 53 ff. However, these statistics do not differentiate between the export of raw and refined sugar. Instead, the latter was converted into raw sugar by adding a weight surcharge. JUCEPLAN, *Boletín Estadístico 1968* (Havana, n.d.), p. 150, and *Boletín Estadístico 1970*, p. 194, do make this qualitative distinction but do not show the regional distribution of sugar exports. If one adds up the Cuban data of the total exports of raw and refined sugar for 1968 (3,323,952 t + 727,156 t = 4,051,109 t), this total deviates only insignificantly from that given in the *Sugar Yearbook*. In my opinion, the difference can be attributed simply to the weight surcharge for refined sugar.

It is more difficult to ascertain reliable data for export revenues. Together with the export volume for raw and refined sugar, JUCEPLAN, *Boletín Estadístico*, also indicates the corresponding total revenues, which amounted to Cub$620 million in 1964. To what extent the various regions or countries participated in this global amount could only be determined if both the prices in foreign currency or the clearing prices and the regional export allocations of raw and refined sugar were available. The pricing terms with the socialist countries for 1964 are not known, and the agreement with the USSR only came into force in 1965.

For 1965–70, I would suggest the following method:

a. The free international market and the USSR only buy raw sugar, the price of which for the USSR is constant at 6.11¢ per pound. On the free international market, the average yearly price for raw sugar is to apply.

b. In the remaining socialist world market both raw and refined sugar is being sold. Quantitative data on these sales at a raw value of 96° sugar are in *Sugar Yearbook*. The revenue from these sales can be assumed to be equal to the difference between the sum of the revenues derived from (a) above and the total revenue of all raw and refined sugar exports shown in JUCEPLAN, *Boletín Estadístico*.

8. *Sugar Yearbook 1970*, p. 52.

9. According to "Lamborn's Chart," the average prices per pound for 96° sugar, raw value, were as follows:

1962	2.97¢	1967	1.99¢
1963	8.48¢	1968	1.98¢
1964	5.86¢	1969	3.37¢
1965	2.21¢	1970	3.75¢
1966	1.86¢	1971	4.52¢

10. Castro, speech of February 24, 1964.

11. Castro, speech of November 27, 1963.

12. Castro, speech of June 7, 1965.

13. See table 17.

14. Castro (speech of May 20, 1970) spoke of an investment volume in the sugar industry totaling Cub$123 million. If the overall figure of Cub$400 million given by Rodriguez ("Informe de la Delegación Cubana") actually was reached, this would still have left an investment amount of Cub$227 million for the agricultural sector of the sugar economy.

15. See chap. 3, n. 9.

16. The assertion that China was willing to pay the same price as the USSR was made by Che Guevara (speech in Algiers, February 22, 1965, in Fidel Castro, Che Guevara, and Regis Debray, *Materialien zur Revolution* [Darmstadt, 1968], p. 142). The source for the COMECON countries, excluding the USSR, is Castro's speech of January 2, 1965.

17. The base data for the computation of revenue realized from sugar sales are summarized in chap. 3, n. 7. In determining export costs, use was made of the weight data on total exports in table 26 and of the average costs per ton of raw sugar in table 27. The possible costs of refining raw sugar were not taken into consideration.

18. Castro predicted favorable production results but was pessimistic about the evolution of the sugar price on the world market (speech of January 2, 1965).

19. Castro, speech of January 21, 1965.

20. FAO, *Commodity Review 1966* (Rome, 1966), p. 99.

21. Castro, speech of January 2, 1965.

22. Hawaiian Sugar Planter's Association, *Sugar Manual 1972* (Honolulu, 1972), p. 33.

23. While rainfall had been above average in 1964, it decreased sharply in 1965 (except in Oriente Province) and, with concomitant high temperatures and the lack of artificial irrigation, was bound to stunt the growth of the sugar cane. Corresponding meteorological data can be found in Roberts, *Cuba 1968,* p. 8.

24. Castro, speeches of May 1 and June 7, 1965.

25. See chap. 3, n. 4.

26. Betancourt, "Harvest Mechanization," p. 41.

27. Castro, speech of April 19, 1966.

28. On January 2, 1965, Castro merely stated that the quantities resulting from

the growth in production were to be sold on the socialist world market. Nevertheless—and despite the continuous stagnation of the free sugar price—it became necessary in the following years to resume selling within the predetermined framework on the free international market.

29. Data from JUCEPLAN, *Boletín Estadístico 1970*, p. 136.

30. According to Hirschmüller and Delavier, the installed capacity for 1968 was still given as 550,000 t/day ("Vor der grossen Zafra," p. 4).

31. Castro, speech of April 19, 1967.

32. Since it had already become apparent in 1966 that, on the basis of previous results, the 10 million-ton harvest could not be reached in 1970, an emergency plan ("peak capacity plan") was set up, according to which the unachieved production increases were to be realized within the next two years (Castro, speech of May 20, 1970). In my opinion, the data given by Martinez in "New Goals" relate to this modified sugar plan.

33. Castro, speech of May 20, 1970.

34. Castro, speech of May 26, 1969.

35. Ibid.

36. Castro, speech of May 20, 1970.

37. In this case, loss in revenue as a result of increased sugar costs. For the first time, computations show the latter to be higher than the sales revenue. In 1969 Cuba clearly produced below the (imaginary) break-even point.

38. Castro, speech of May 26, 1969.

39. JUCEPLAN, *Boletín Estadístico 1970*, p. 54; in round figures.

40. Castro, speech of May 20, 1970.

41. Castro, speech of February 9, 1970.

42. Castro, speech of May 20, 1970.

43. Ibid.

44. Daily reports were issued on the progress of the harvest. The present data, therefore, are based on *Granma* from November 1969 to July 1970.

45. Castro, speech of May 19, 1970.

46. According to Castro (speech of May 26, 1969), an average of 100,000 workers were employed by the sugar industry alone. On December 9, 1970, he revealed that this figure had risen to over 120,000 workers (while the processing capacity remained the same as in the 1960s), a fact which he cited as an example of the drop in labor productivity.

47. Castro, speech of May 20, 1970.

48. Castro, speech of May 19, 1970.

49. This computation is based on the assumption that in this case an industrial yield of 12 percent could have been maintained, comparable to the one achieved with larger *zafras* of the past.

50. Castro, speech of February 2, 1970. But as early as 1966, Castro had pointed out (in his speech of April 19) that irrespective of an increase in sugar production, the rest of the economy was not to be neglected.

51. The concept of a "break-even point" may appear somewhat irrelevant in this

context. It refers to the point on a quantity graph known in production theory where the total costs curve intersects the total revenue curve.

52. JUCEPLAN, *Boletín Estadístico 1968*, p. 150, and *Boletín Estadístico 1970*, p. 194.

53. Castro, speech of July 26, 1970.

54. This refers both to primary products and to by-products, and therefore includes all raw materials (JUCEPLAN, *Boletín Estadístico 1970*, pp. 192 ff.).

55. For more detailed data, see ibid., pp. 197 ff.

56. JUCEPLAN, *Boletín Estadístico 1970*, pp. 190 ff. The basic principles for the market classification were drawn up by the author on the basis of Cuban foreign trade statistics. See also JUCEPLAN, *Boletín Estadístico 1968*, pp. 148 ff.

57. United Nations, Supplement to *World Trade Annual 1967* (New York, 1971), vol. 2, pp. 235 ff.

58. This assumption appears valid on the premise that Cuba did not dispose of any foreign currency reserves and that it was not possible to transfer the export surplus from markets of type 2 in the amount of $126 million to markets of type 1, since these net reserves were merely cleared through accounting operations. If these two premises should be in error, the credit volume would have to be corrected downward.

59. Detailed data on the Soviet trade with Cuba are in "Vneshnaya torgovlya soyuza SSR za 1968 god," *Mezhdunarodnye otnosheniya* (Moscow, 1969).

60. Castro, speech of January 3, 1973. The agreement provided for a moratorium on repayment and interest of all credits granted by the USSR to Cuba before 1972. These debts were then to be settled between 1985 and 2010.

61. This figure corresponds to the cumulative negative balance in Cuba's trade with the socialist nations that are not members of COMECON between 1963 and 1970.

62. "Sbornik deystuyushchikh dogovory, soglasheniy i konventsiy, zaklyvt-sennikh SSSR s innostrannymi gosudarstvami, vyp XXIV. Izd-vo 'Mezhduna-rodnye otnosheniya'; 1971," p. 210, quoted in A. D. Bekarevic and M. M. Kud-raev, "Sovetski Soyuz i Kuba," *Ekonomicheskoe sotrudnichestvo* (Moscow, 1973), p. 224.

63. For the Western world market this was based on the median sugar price in 1968 ($43.70/t), and for the USSR on the agreed clearing price (Cub$143.88/t). The quantity of raw sugar compensating one ton of the given product was then multiplied by the Cuban sugar costs (1968 = Cub$91.35/t).

64. The Cuban import statistics show quantities and costs of goods, but not their regional distribution (JUCEPLAN, *Boletín Estadístico 1968*, pp. 152 ff.). Therefore, only raw materials could be selected for which the Cuban import quantities corresponded to Soviet export quantities ("Vneshnaya torgovlya," pp. 288 ff.). On this premise, the Soviet Union held an import monopoly, so that corresponding prices could be ascertained from *Boletín Estadístico*. However, the concordance of Soviet and Cuban statistics is only fragmentary, so that this may be a source of error.

65. Omitted from consideration are additional grants to Cuba, for example, those from international organizations and the sizable aid in armaments from the USSR.

66. Bekarevic and Kudraev, "Sovetski Soyuz i Kuba," p. 192.

67. Castro (speech of June 4, 1963) mentioned a price of 4¢ per pound.

68. A well-documented report on Cuban employment policy is Carmelo Mesa-Lago's *Labor Force, Employment, Unemployment and Underemployment in Cuba: 1899–1970* (Beverly Hills: Sage Publications, 1972).

69. ECLA, *Economic Survey of Latin America, 1963*, p. 263, quoted in Mesa-Lago, *Labor Force*, p. 53.

70. Castro, speech of September 2, 1970.

71. Delegación de Cuba, XI Conferencia Regional de la FAO, *Dos años de desarrollo agropecuario cubano 1968–1970* (Caracas, 1970), p. 5.

72. Ibid., p. 7.

73. Castro, speech of March 13, 1968.

74. Roberts, *Cuba 1968*, p. 209.

75. Quantities of fertilizer produced and imported, from JUCEPLAN, *Boletín Estadistico 1970*, pp. 144, 202–03. Quantities of cement produced and imported, from ibid., pp. 150, 204–05. Development of the construction industry as a whole from ibid., p. 164, and, particularly in the sector of cane cultivation, p. 162.

76. With the technical and financial assistance of Great Britain and the USSR, two fertilizer plants with a total production capacity of 700,000 tons were under construction in 1970 in Cienfuegos and Nuevitas, but both encountered delays in completion (Delegación de Cuba, *Dos años de desarrollo*, p. 24). Similar efforts were made in the cement industry with the assistance of the GDR and Czechoslovakia, but no plants were in production by 1970. As far as I could determine from conversations with foreign experts in Cuba, the reasons for the delays were chiefly in management and in the lack of professional competence among Cuban coworkers.

77. Table 34 would seem to contradict this assessment. As shown here, activity increased by 42 percent as of 1968, compared to 1962. My own observations in 1972 left the impression that the cities had been neglected in favor of infrastructure in the provinces. After 1970, housing construction was again promoted more actively.

78. Regarding the concept of national income and its computation, see Erich Klinkmüller, "Nationaleinkommen (NE.), Volkseinkommen (VE.)," in *Wörterbuch zur politischen Oekonomie*, ed. Gert von Einem (Opladen, 1973), p. 246.

79. The population of Cuba grew from 7.1 million (1962) to 8.1 million (1968) (JUCEPLAN, *Boletín Estadistico 1968*, p. 8).

80. Castro, speech of July 26, 1970.

81. Production figures for agriculture and industry are taken from JUCEPLAN, *Boletín Estadistico 1970*, pp. 97, 144 ff.

82. See in this connection Carmelo Mesa-Lago, who attempts to trace empirically the evolution of this rapprochement ("Conversion of the Cuban Economy to Soviet Orthodoxy," *Journal of Economic Issues*, 8, no. 1 [March 1974]:41 ff.).

Bibliography

Anuario azucarero de Cuba 1962. Havana, n.d.

Baran, Paul. *The Political Economy of Growth.* New York: Monthly Review Press, 1957.

Barkin, David. "Agricultura: El sector clave del desarrollo de Cuba." *Economía y Desarrollo,* no. 3 (July–September 1970):45 ff.

Bekarevic, A. D., and Kudraev, M. M. "Sovetski Soyuz i Kuba." *Ekonomicheskoe sotrudnichestvo.* Moscow, 1973.

Betancourt, Armando. "Harvest Mechanization and Its Effects on Cane Quality." *CubaAzúcar* (July–September 1970):39 ff.

–––––––. "Study in Extraneous Matter in Sugar Cane." *CubaAzúcar* (September–December 1966):80 ff.

Bianchi, Andrés. "Agriculture." In *Cuba: The Economic and Social Revolution,* ed. Dudley Seers, pp. 65–150. Chapel Hill: University of North Carolina Press, 1964.

Blackburn, Robin. "The Economics of the Cuban Revolution." In *Latin America and the Caribbean,* ed. Claudio Veliz, pp. 622–31. New York: Praeger, 1968.

Boorstein, Edward. *The Economic Transformation of Cuba.* New York: Monthly Review Press, 1968.

Botî, Regino. "El plan de desarrollo económico de 1962." *Cuba Socialista,* 1, no. 4 (December 1961):19 ff.

Boynton, Maryanna. "Effects of Embargo and Boycott: The Cuban Case." Ph.D. dissertation, University of California at Riverside, 1972.

"Caracteristicas y organisación de la industria azucarera cubana." *CubaAzúcar* (July–August 1967):21 ff.

Castro, Fidel. "La historia me absolverá: Defensa en el juicio por el asalto al Cuartel Moncada en Santiago de Cuba." In idem, *Pensamiento politico, economico y social,* pp. 3 ff. Havana, n.d.

Castro, Fidel. Speeches from 1963 to 1970. Direct broadcasts of Radio Havana, Radio Progreso, and Radio Liberación, published by Servicio de Monitoring del Colegio Nacional de Taquigrafas de Cuba en Exilio, Miami, quoted from the reference material of the Central Library of the University of Pittsburgh, Pittsburgh, Pa. The speeches were published on the following working day in *Revolución* (organ of the 26th of July Movement) and *Hoy* (organ of the Partido Socialista Popular). After October 4, 1965, they were published in the central organ of the PCC, *Granma.* After January 1966, *Granma* was published also as a weekly in Spanish, French, and English. From that time on, I have used the publication date of the speech in *Granma Weekly Review (GWR)*; the texts are identical with those of the Monitoring Service.

Quotations from the following speeches have been used: June 4, November 27, 1963; January 2, February 24, October 10, October 31, 1964; January 2, January 21, May 1, June 7, 1965; April 19, 1966 (*GWR*, April 24, 1966); April 19, 1967 (*GWR*, April 30, 1967); January 2 (*GWR*, January 7), March 13 (*GWR*, March 24), July 26, 1968 (*GWR*, July 28, 1968); May 26 (*GWR*, June 1), October 27, 1969 (*GWR*, November 2, 1969); February 2 (*GWR*, February 15), February 9 (*GWR*, February 15), May 19 (*GWR*, May 31), May 20 (*GWR*, May 31), July 26 (*GWR*, August 2), September 2 (*GWR*, September 20), December 7, 1970 (*GWR*, December 20, 1970); January 3, 1973 (*GWR*, January 14, 1973).

CEPAL. *Estudio Económico de America Latina 1963*. New York, 1964.

Chonchol, Jacques. "Analisis crítico de la reforma agraria cubana." *El Trimestre Económico*, 30, no. 117 (January–March 1963):69–143.

Cuban Economic Research Project of the University of Miami, Florida. *Cuba: Agriculture and Planning*. Coral Gables, 1965.

————. *Study on Cuba*. Coral Gables, 1965.

Current Digest of the Soviet Press. Vol. 5, no. 4 (1964).

Delegación de Cuba, XI Conferencia Regional de la FAO. *Dos años de desarrollo agropecuario cubano 1968–1970*. Caracas, 1970.

"El desarrollo industrial de Cuba." *Cuba Socialista*, nos. 56, 57 (April, May 1966):128 ff., 94 ff.

Dorticos, Osvaldo. "Avances institucionales de la revolución." *Cuba Socialista*, 6, no. 53 (January 1966):2–23.

Draper, Theodore. *Castroism: Theory and Practice*. New York: Praeger, 1965.

Dumont, René. *Cuba est-il socialiste?* Paris, 1970.

————. *Cuba: Socialisme et développement*. Paris, 1964.

Economic Commission for Latin America. *Economic Survey of Latin America, 1963*. New York, 1965.

"La experiencia de Cuba en comercio exterior." *Comercio Exterior* (April–June 1964):50 ff.

Food and Agriculture Organization. "Agricultural Commodities Projections for 1970." Special Supplement to *FAO Commodity Review 1962*. Rome, 1962.

————. *Commodity Review 1966*. Rome, 1966.

————. *Agricultural Commodities Projections 1970–1980*. Vol. 2. Rome, 1971.

Frank, André Gunder. *Capitalism and Underdevelopment in Latin America*. New York: Monthly Review Press, 1969.

Guevara, Ernesto Che. "On Production Costs and the Budgetary System," "On the Budgetary Finance System," and "Man and Socialism in Cuba." In *Man and Socialism in Cuba*, ed. Bertram Silverman, pp. 113–21, 122–56, 337–54. New York: Atheneum, 1971.

————. Speech in Algiers, February 22, 1965. In Castro, Fidel; Guevara, Che; and Debray, Regis. *Materialien zur Revolution*, pp. 138 ff. Darmstadt, 1968.

Gutelman, Michel. *L'Agriculture socialisée à Cuba.* Paris, 1967.

Hagelberg, Gerhard. "Strukturwandlungen in der Weltzuckerwirtschaft seit 1960." In *Jahrbuch für Wirtschaftsgeschichte 1969/IV*, pp. 99 ff. Berlin, 1969.

Hawaii, State of, Department of Planning and Economic Development. *The Sugar Industry in Hawaii.* Research Report No. 72–2. Honolulu, 1973.

Higgins, Benjamin. *Economic Development: Problems, Principles and Policies*, 2d edition. New York: Norton, 1968.

Hirschman, Albert. *The Strategy of Economic Development.* New Haven: Yale University Press, 1958.

Hirschmüller, H., and Delavier, H. J. "Vor der grossen Zafra. Die Zuckerwirtschaft Kubas 10 Jahre nach der Revolution." In *Zeitschrift für Zuckerindustrie*, 1969, installment 2, pp. 74 ff. Berlin, 1969.

Huberman, Leo, and Sweezy, Paul. *Socialism in Cuba.* New York: Monthly Review Press, 1969.

International Sugar Council, ed. *The World Sugar Economy: Structure and Policies.* Vol. 1, *National Sugar Economies and Policies*, vol. 2, *The World Picture.* London, 1963.

_____. *Sugar Yearbook 1960.* London, 1961.

International Sugar Organization, ed. *Sugar Yearbook 1970.* London, 1971.

JUCEPLAN (Junta Central de Planificación). "La planificación económica en Cuba." In *Aspectos administrativos de la planificación: Documentos de un seminario.* Havana, n.d.

_____. *Boletín Estadístico 1968, 1970, 1971.* Havana, n.d.

Klinkmüller, Erich. "Nationaleinkommen (NE.), Volkseinkommen (VE.)." In *Wörterbuch zur politischen Oekonomie*, ed. Gert von Einem, pp. 246 ff. Opladen, 1973.

"Lamborn's Chart of World Sugar Prices 1931–1971." In *Sugar Manual 1972*, ed. Hawaiian Sugar Planter's Association, p. 32. Honolulu, 1972.

Lataste, Albán. *Cuba: ¿hacia una nueva economía política del socialismo?* Santiago de Chile, 1968.

Lorenz, Detlef. "Zur Typologie der Entwicklungsländer." In *Entwicklungsländer*, ed. Bruno Fritsch. Cologne and Berlin, 1968.

Lowy, Michael. *The Marxism of Che Guevara.* New York: Monthly Review Press, 1973.

Martinez, Tomás. "New Goals in the Development of the Cuban Sugar Industry." *CubaAzúcar* (May–July 1967):40 ff.

Mesa-Lago, Carmelo. "Availability and Reliability of Statistics in Socialist Cuba." *Latin American Research Review*, 4 (Spring and Summer, 1969).

_____. "Economic Policies and Growth." In *Revolutionary Change in Cuba*, ed. idem, pp. 277–338. Pittsburgh: University of Pittsburgh Press, 1971.

_____. *The Labor Force, Employment, Unemployment and Underemployment in Cuba: 1899–1970.* Beverly Hills: Sage Publications, 1972.

_____. "Conversion of the Cuban Economy to Soviet Orthodoxy." *Journal of Economic Issues*, 8, no. 1 (March 1974):41 ff.

Mollett, J. A. "Capital in Hawaiian Sugar: Its Formation and Relation to Labor and Output, 1870–1957." *Agricultural Economics Bulletin*. Honolulu, June 1961.

Nolff, Max. *The Origins of Socialism in Cuba*. Ithaca, N.Y.: Cornell University Press, 1970.

Noticias Económicas, 5, no. 40. Havana, 1969.

O'Connor, James. *The Origins of Socialism in Cuba*. Ithaca: Cornell University Press, 1970.

Roberts, Paul, ed. *Cuba 1968*. Supplement to *Statistical Abstract of Latin America*. Los Angeles: University of California Latin American Center, 1970.

Rodas, Ricardo. "Aplicación de las tablas insumo-producto al sector industrial cubano." *Comercio Exterior*, 2 (July–September 1964):2 ff.

Rodriguez, Carlos Rafael. "Informe de la Delegación Cubana al XV período de sesiones de la Conferencia de la FAO, Roma 1969." *Economía y Desarrollo*, no. 1 (January–March 1970):2–30.

Romeo, Carlos. "Acerca del desarrollo económica de Cuba." *Cuba Socialista*, 5, no. 52 (December 1965):2–24.

Seers, Dudley, ed. *Cuba: The Economic and Social Revolution*. Chapel Hill: University of North Carolina Press, 1964.

Statistisches Jahrbuch für die Bundesrepublik Deutschland 1972. Stuttgart and Mainz, 1972.

Sturrock, Ford. "Sugar Beet or Sugar Cane?" *Journal of Agricultural Economics*, 20, no. 1 (1969).

United Nations. Supplement to *WorldTrade Annual 1967*. Vol. 2. New York, 1971.

Viton, A., and Pignalosa, F. *Trends and Forces in World Sugar Consumption*. FAO Commodity Bulletin Series, no. 32. Rome, 1961.

"Vneshnaya torgovlya soyuza SSR za 1968 god." *Mezhdunarodnye otnosheniya*. Moscow, 1969.

Index

Agricultural yield, 46, 83; defined, 142n11
Agriculture, 134–35; diversification of, 21–22, 31–32, 33, 37
Army, 90, 93–94
Association of Small Farmers, 29

Backwardness, technological, 11, 39
Balance of payments, 34, 90–91
Baran, Paul, 25
Beets, sugar, 9
Break-even point, 95, 109; defined, 154n51
Bureaucratization, 135–36

Cane, sugar, 6
Castro, Fidel, 38, 55, 68, 80, 82, 94, 105, 108, 127–28, 134
Central Bank, 31
Centros de acopio, 70, 90, 94, 97
China, 14, 53, 85, 120
COMECON, 18–19, 62
Commonwealth Sugar Agreement, 18
Consciousness-raising, 30
Consumption, of sugar, 11–15, 49. See also individual countries
Costs, of sugar production, computation of, 57–62, 85–86
Council for Mutual Economic Aid, 18–19, 62
Cuba: geography of, 4; natural resources of, 4; population of, 4; climate of, 4–5, 6, 153n23; consumption of sugar in, 55, 81

Cuban-Soviet trade agreements, 55, 120, 125

Dependency, 3
Depreciation, 60–61
Distribution of income, 23–24, 135, 143n27. See also Redistribution
Diversification, 3; of agriculture, 21–22, 31–32, 33, 37; of exports, 109
Dualism, technological, 23

ECLA, 127
EEC, 18
EFTA, 50
Elasticity of demand, 13
Empresas Consolidadas, 31
Engels' law, 13
European Economic Community, 18
European Free Trade Association, 50
Export-oriented economy, 5, 6, 11, 22
Export revenue, 89, 91, 94–95, 97–98, 99, 101, 106; computation of, 62–63, 152n7
Exports, 24; structure of, 9, 19–21, 26, 32, 81; computation of, 152n7
Extraction rate, defined, 8

FAO, 13, 33, 48, 91, 142n12
Fertilizer, 68, 102
Food and Agriculture Organization. See FAO
Food, importation of, 22, 110
Foreign trade, structure of, 9, 19–21, 26, 32, 81

161

PITT LATIN AMERICAN SERIES
Cole Blasier, Editor

Revolutionary Change in Cuba
Carmelo Mesa-Lago, Editor

Cloth, ISBN 0-8229-3232-6, $16.95
Paper, ISBN 0-8229-5244-0, $4.50

Selected Latin American One-Act Plays
Francesca Colecchia and Julio Matas, Editors and Translators

Paper, ISBN 0-8229-5241-6, $3.95

Society and Education in Brazil
Robert J. Havighurst and J. Roberto Moreira

Paper, ISBN 0-8229-5207-6, $2.95

All prices are subject to change without notice. Order from your bookstore or the publisher.

UNIVERSITY OF PITTSBURGH PRESS
Pittsburgh, Pa. 15260